# Birch Philosopher X

*by*

# Red Washburn

*Finishing Line Press*
Georgetown, Kentucky

# Birch Philosopher X

Publisher: Leah Huete de Maines

Editor: Christen Kincaid

Cover Art: Adriana Varella

Author Photo: Morgan Gwenwald

Cover Design: Elizabeth Maines McCleavy


Order online: www.finishinglinepress.com
                also available on amazon.com

Author inquiries and mail orders:
Finishing Line Press
P. O. Box 1626
Georgetown, Kentucky 40324
U. S. A.

# Table of Contents

## VII.

## VIII.

## IX.

## X.

*Acknowledgements/Credits*

*For Colleen Washburn (3/14/1951-9/25/2020)—*
*I could never steal enough daisies for you.*

*For Bernadette McGuire (5/8/1928-3/5/2011)—*
*I could never smuggle in enough Milky Ways for you.*

*For Lux and Volt—*
*Thanks for tucking me in with your purrs.*

I.

# Tit-Bucket and Denim

***

*Genderbathe*

On the ground, lights dim above me, gongs vibrating all around me, the mat is under me, I swim in the vibrations like currents. Reverberations on walls like water drops on arm hairs, I am smothered in the safe—the closest to it. Surrounded in the sonic and suffocated by the gravity, I swallow the surfs. Arms outstretched, binder liquid-latexed, weightless and topless, I listen to the crash of symbols like waves. Inhale in the metal, exhale out the salt, breathe in and out, the in between.

***

*It's Chinatown*

I stretch out on the wood floor in front of a massive window. I feel the ground on my back. I feel the mat and pillow cushion, my curled fingers, and knotted neck. I feel my head getting lighter. I pull the blanket over my body. I look at the buildings, the birds, and the clouds. I close my eyes. I hear shamanic drumming, tuning forks, gongs, Himalayan singing bowls, chimes, percussion, and among other sounds, even those that trigger like snores. I inhale through my nose deeply, and let it all out through my mouth. I am in and out of brainwaves from waking state to alpha and theta states. I almost fall sleep. I focus more on my breath. I am swimming in fresh mountain water. I soak in it, my skin slurping it up from freckle to freckle. I see the bubbles. I imagine walking with my shirt off, my chest nonexistent, and arms out, sucking down the wind, with my cats trailing behind me in the green. I open my eyes. I see the clouds moving on my chest. I see my face in my recovery bed. I hear the sounds of the gong blasting out enemies in castle halls, the ground up and up.

***

*Liberation Day*

I woke up to my tits in a bucket. I asked where they would go beforehand, as if I gave a shit. My surgeon told me they would be in there, then sent out for biopsies, and ultimately, mere rubbish, what they were in my mind. No

1

piercings, "AH" inked below both sides of my collarbone, she kicked out my friends, whispering to me to lie down and "take a deep breath and take a nice nap," as she held my hand goodnight. She was guiding me where I wanted to be, neither girl, nor boy, just mowing the lawn shirtless with my dad before I was told to put on a t-shirt at puberty. On July 31, 2018, I went under fast and came out faster. I felt like a horse kicked me in the chest. Every move pushed into knives, my bloody mummy gauze below me, bloody fallopian drains in my sides, and bloody cauliflower bolster dressings peeking out. I could feel where the scalpel was dragged and the drains cut and rammed into my sides. I could not feel my free nipple grafts, though I thought about a mini Slasherfest there, too. I imagined bike chains mangling my chest, mushrooms being cut for nipple grafts, and cyborgs tunneling tubes inside the sides of the body like a tin can telephone. I ripped open my blue plaid gown in the front, examining my flat chest, smiled, put on my leopard baseball cap, looked out the window at the Hudson, and thought about how I was the luckiest trans fuck to be alive.

I sat up, had the nurse unhook my fluids, and went to pee. I recall the lightness in my gait, the freedom in my drug-induced swag, and the cart I pulled to my side being a caravan of unicorns from the fat bags that used to sit on my chest. I slid back in bed, staring at the waves, floating in this weightlessness to meet my grandmother for a tea party decades back in time. I waited for my chosen fams, friends, and my ex to join me. They rolled in with side hugs, forehead kisses, and boredom-free gifts. They were there with and for me when I did not want to wake up to the wrong name, the wrong pronoun, the wrong me, anymore than I did in the wrong binary body I lived in for much of my life. I had pasta and more pasta, and then went back to sleep, no dreams, because they were real now—or as real as they can be if we exist.

I went home with a friend to the feline reunion and a flooded apartment with pantyhose strapped around my neck, first-class top surgery genderfucking action there. I wanted to pick my cats up. They kept climbing up my legs and walking on my chest, and I never wanted their purrs in my ears and pads imprinting my chest more. I crouched down to their level, pet them hand over hand, sweet talked them, and kissed their little heads. I went outside in my yard, looked up my favorite cardinal tree, and took my first flat chest picture. I felt the wind under my shirt. I went inside, jerked off, and cried for the connection I now experienced but had longed for in my own body for so long. I fell asleep on my back with my cats on my sides like bookends.

For a solid week, I emptied drains, charted fluid volume, eyed red, orange, and yellow discharge. I monitored leaks and drain clogs, freak-outs occurring minimally. My trans friend and friend's daughter, a medical student, helped me change my gauze the first few times, both of them experts in this line of work. I laughed at my fear of ripping open my double incisions or losing a nipple with them there, them telling me stories of a friend watching their nipple go down the drain and the drain wrapping around a closet doorknob and blood spraying in the bedroom. The worst part of surgery was not showering for a week and not picking up my cats for three months, but my care crew made it better. I spent a lot of time shirtless with them doing photo shoots. I did them in front of academic books and anarchist cats. I even did them outside with vegan-friendly mosquitos tearing into me. I learned to enjoy my post-op body as it healed in all its grossness, yet I immediately felt like the epochs of carrying bricks, double-shirting, side covering, and binding them were a distant memory. I got my drains out after a week of agony and annoyingness. I will never forget that that moment of ripping and soothing, the snake under my chest, biting its way out to be strangled and hurled into the trash, and yet the peace restored in me while my body was at war. I looked at myself in the mirror there, turning from one side to the other, scratching my head, and smiling at myself. I danced all the way down the street. I write shirtless a lot, with water next to me, not whiskey, and yet my party nip is still out in full force.

***

*Behind Sugarloaf*

I tear off my t-shirt, climb down the ladder into the dark water in my shorts, shades, and baseball cap, hop into the red kayak. I leave the yellow life jacket strapped in with the patriarchy and what I am told it has done to me by butches who fought the cops at Stonewall on this lesbian separatist land before peacing out. When I left, I carried this feeling into the airport, where TSA dicks grabbed my junk. Now I let my new nipples guide me down the canal. This is the first time I have been kayaking without tits, let alone without a shirt on. I take the oar, paddle softly, and play hide and seek with the yellow crowned night heron. They soar in between the mangled tree roots, the snakes bobbing, and the driftwood floating. I feel the sun on my back, the wind on my chest scars, and flow into the lake. Low to the water, the ripples on my hands and the fossils on my feet, I raise my shaved head and watch the hawks glide above me. They fly with rain pelting their wings and waves slapping the kayak—out far, in before long—knowing how to return, though not going back. The imminent storm hardens my nips and reddens my incisions, yet my goosebumps become raised fists and pruned fingers become guns. In the still out here on no man's/no woman's land, I rock back and forth, roam with my breath, and feel free.

## She Doesn't Want to Be She Anymore

she takes off the "S."
then her right breast.
she takes off the "H."
then her left breast.
she keeps the "E."
she doesn't want to be "she" anymore.

she's too queer.
she's too trans.
she's too hairy.
she's too poor.
she's too "she."
she doesn't want to be "she" anymore.

she wants to be "E."

she takes off the "S."
then her right breast.
she takes off the "H."
then her left breast.
she keeps the "E."
she doesn't want to be "she" anymore.

she's a bitch.
she's a cunt.
she's a slut.
she's a dick.
she's a tranny.
she's a freak.
she doesn't want to be "she" anymore.

she wants to be "E."

she takes off the "S."
then her right breast.
she takes off the "H."
then her left breast.

she keeps the "E."
she doesn't want to be "she" anymore.
she wants to be "E."

she cuts her nails.
she grows out her pits.
she wears a beard.
she shaves her head.
she inks her skin.
she doesn't want to be "she" anymore.

she wants to be "E."

she takes off the "S."
then her right breast.
she takes off the "H."
then her left breast.
she keeps the "E."
she doesn't want to be "she" anymore.

she wants to be "E."

she wants to cut off her tits.
she has a knife pointing to her chest.
she has a pen in her hand.
She writes her name.

They write "E."

# Power, or Point of Zoo

*(for Leslie Feinberg)*

June Jordan said, "There is power and there is point of view, and whoever has power determines the point of view."

I am face down on a filthy table in a Thai massage place in my boxers and socks. I think about my jeans, t-shirt, binder, leather jacket, sneakers, and baseball cap hanging on the door and block out the man's grunts above me. I close my eyes and grind my teeth while a straight cis dude beats the shit of me there. How did I get to a point where stranger's hands are on me—a man's, no less—so that I can feel human again? I instruct him to go deep—that is all the matters to me now. I can feel his elbow in my shoulder blades, his knees on my lower back, his fists pounding my upper back, and his fingers digging into my neck's trigger points. I breathe through a hole encased by a smelly, yellow towel. I feel the bruises. I think about the sound of her voice as she calls me my deadname and reignites my trauma, the refusals to meet with me to do feminist work, the threatening tone of her words at my request to respect my gender identity, and the henchmen who smile at me as they conspire with her to bar me from doing the work I created. I think about commander-in-thief proclaiming "grab them by the pussy," allowing states to choose where gender non-conforming people can piss, and banning trans folks from the military rather than banning the military industrial complex itself. I think about the sound of violence as I listen for the echoes of my tears on the floor beneath me, where that same towel should sit before spin. I release the power she and the state have on my body, although I am deeply aware of my white privilege here, for just one hour before I find new tools to build up my inner warrior, because what other choice do we have? As Leslie Feinberg says in "Transgender Liberation: A Movement Whose Times Has Come," "We are the class that does the work of the world, and can revolutionize it. We can win true liberation."

# Tr@ns Circuits

*(with Adriana Varella)*


colonizing circuits
explode without electric singularities questioning empires
maps that pop when inflamed patriarchal
knives on chests like flags in the dirt appropriate the objects of power
a middle finger in a breeder cunt using different dicks
cum in and on dildos desire
to be clitoral extensions shoot moans across countries
each day mini dicks grow more
reach for the space between tree and cloud the wind sighs like kites
more fuck, more grow
free that switches on with a snap

————————


circuits of illusion
gait that skips backwards in mindfold.
about whom? I was starting to disappear become a nothing fog that spits hail
i started to experiment be a man in a world of privileges imagine a world where
you choose who you are
when no one exists
and be able to stay in yourself without being pestered by others palming beards
manspread the binary
homeworks.
dot the scan, emotional bleeding ghosts servant I have freed myself
connect spots, yellowing

————————————————————————————————————————————

ideological circuits
liminalize thought and meaning divergent
from all patriarchal world to trans ideology institutions legislate beings
into unbeings, undoings of humans,

macro beef, micro.

————————

sexual circuits

crygasm rooms with colored negatives try to penetrate many asses

trans language

I don't understand. (the source of it, the poem,
of it).
Is it better if I understand or if I don't?
Google translate is open in Portuguese.

# Psithurism in X Minor

Canoes piled up on the grass, they look into what was once water. It was the water they learned the breaststroke, the water that wrapped algae around their leg, water that hid a washer their best friend banged her knee against, that they biked along to see the ducks, and that iced-held their sleds in the winter. No lifeguards needed anymore, they stand on the green lawn-lake and look into the void of it. They have been gentrified out like the beavers. From that mud into which they squeezed their toes, they grew up into something else—the paddle that does not have a point of origin, a return, and a destination—a tree, under which they pee with their shirt off. They look up at the leaves swaying low like their voice, and think this is like transition, a girlhood like a deadname, a gender like an imagination.

\*\*\*

Under them, she grabs their cock with her cunt. Her strength is around them. They tell her they can feel her. They lift her legs higher and dig deeper into her like hands in the sand. They cum-shake inside her, their chest turns red, she caresses their scars, and they sink between her legs, throbbing harder with their tongue on her clit, inside her, and sucking her lips, their beard soaked in her. She tells them to lie beside her, and she welcomes in their fist, their cock still hard for her. She grabs their Jeans Pocket and jerks it gently. They close their eyes. They think that she might just get their gender before they take off one of their dicks—like a barber who grabs the blade and goes high and tight on the fade before they ask for it.

\*\*\*

Around their head, flew a firefly. It lit up the dark bedroom, looming around them. It flew above their chest scars, zig zagged along them in the AC, and then bobbed across their cat's whiskers. To be on the inside with all that fire when it was supposed to be outside, it seemed wild, they thought, while they were trying to sleep. Their eyes slow blinked and then traced—engulfed by this blaze. They thought they would dream in this glow, but they got up, cupped this life, and set it to the night wind. They thought about all the fireflies who reminded them to how to provide their own light, roam about, glide near the trees, and be free. They preferred to let their cat chase away their bad dreams.

# Mx. Meyer's

They were waiting. They talked to their vet about their cat's insulin dose, with him affirming that they were a good mom and with hesitation, then, a good dad. They were still waiting for insurance coverage, for doctor's approval of medical relevance, and pharmacy availability. They reflected on the routine misadventures in misgendering. They drove to two drug stores, with needles, syringes, and testosterone strapped in the passenger seat. They carried it around for miles as if it were a person. They quivered as their partner shot it into them, her red nails on their stomach—femme labor—feeling it take a long swim in the subcutaneous. They put their used T needles with Lux's used diabetes needles. They like that they are bonded in this way. They wonder if their vet will notice their gender in the laundry detergent dispensary. They are waiting.

II.

# 156 Avenue and Madison Road

The long, dirt road with tractor marks welcomes her home. She blasts "Amazon Womyn," belts out the Tribe lyrics, watches the ferns sway, and admires the hand-made Fest signs leading to the gate. Sisters greet her, and almost immediately, her shoulders drop and her breath slows. A womon takes off her shirt in the parking lot. Two miles down another womon sneezes and a sister says "God bless you" five miles past Lois Lane. Another womon lends her truck to a sister who is unable to unload herself. Forty womyn help push a broken down tractor, while others greet, "Welcome home, sister." After a fourteen-hour drive, she already feels revived just being here.

***

She has done this pilgrimage five times. In each, the female energy affirms and heals her each time. Every festival has its own ethos for her: the first, she grieved her beloved grandmother and honored her ancestors; the second, she quit an exploitive job and accepted her butch/ genderqueer identity; the third, she acknowledged an unfulfilling marriage and identified creative alienation; the fourth, she accepted ending her long-term relationship and coped with her new girlfriend's coming out process; and the fifth and final, helped her embrace love and mourn the festival, the last of which remains one of the important moments of her life.

2011

It was just after her grandmother died. Her grandmother taught her how to be on her own and create her own life, like fest builds its womyn-run city from the stages to the showers. Her legacy was with her when Bernice Johnson Reagon sang "Sometimes" with her daughter Toshi Reagon. She pondered the generations of womyn in mother-daughter-granddaughter relationships with values of kindness, respect, acceptance, and love. She thought one could never have enough grandmothers. Their voices traveled down her spine and up to her eyes. Her tears fell down her freezing face onto the crisp ground, where they drew eyebrows in the dirt like worms coming up for air during a rainstorm. She sees a Monarch looming above her, her mouth opens, and she inhales the space between them, where the past and present meet.

***

With Treeano in the foreground (now tattooed on her arm), she then watched the sisters lift the lanterns into the black sky as a gift to the sisters who are now stars. The sage unites and heals her. Passing sister-stars look over the womyn dancing to the drum beats in the firepit and shine down on the glow sticks on Easy Street. They are free to roam until the flashlights go out. She hears womyn howling at the moon after the witches conclude their ceremony. She later thinks about them, as she leaves the showers, with just a towel over her neck, feeling the lanterns' heat on her body and seeing the steam rise. With each step towards their tent decorated with their own glow, she kicks up dust, feels her locs freezing up, and sighs softly to the moon for the ash-sisters, the shadow-gait of her spirit.

## 2012

It is a place where her inner freak belongs. It is a place where she does not have to look back on Womonly Way in the dark. It is a place where she does not carry a knife. It is a place where she does not break faces. It is a place where she shaves her face across from the Janes in Amazon Acres. It is a place where she lets blood drip down her legs in the Triangle shower. A place where she brushes the wisps of hair atop her freshly shaved head with a fork. A place where she does not get hard stares or double takes. A place where she does not get snickers or finger-pointing. A place where she does not get "sir, ma'am, sir." Where a man does not flirt with her girl in front of her. Where her voice does not crack. Where she does not get mansplained about her own work. Where she swaggers around crafts bare-chested like she did as a kid but without the stretch marks and half-sleeves. Where she nods, smiles, and says "hello" to a stranger on the dish line. It is a place where she is seen and heard.

## 2013

She started looking up the Acoustic Stage's tree-skirt that summer. The tree waves "hello," clapping energetically for the deaf womyn, who use their hands to hear the leaves talk. She would hit the ground during her security shift without looking down like collapsing with whiskey on her breath, replaying Shelley Nicole's mantra, "when you are on the ground, you can get back up." She was with her, but she was not with herself. She would imagine another non-her she had not-met yet. She would trace branches with her hazel eyes like connecting zit scars up her small back. She would soar through to the open blue like bumblebees through womyn's beard clouds. She would block out words for chirps like her long, dark hair shielding vision from the orange-flamed sun. She would feel grounded with her chest to the sap stank above for the first time since she started dirt-hugging the layers that separated those who could trim nails from those who could not. She would let her litanies of "what ifs" slow-drift like womyn's voices in the Green Space. She sees no trash to pick up, no equipment was stolen, and no able-bodied womyn using the DART Jane. She watches a grasshopper on her sneaks. She does move, even with guitars.

She holds space, like rocks on words, already breathed-etched into the black air. She learns how to breathe, inhaling so her shoulder blades shift the dusty earth into the slow blow. She detaches under the tree's denim cuffs, a billet-doux with a woo.

2014

She was done. She dragged along her feet along Lois' earth like they were attached to the watermelon tree. She opened her mouth hard like she saw a cop upon re-entering. She knocked into people like she drummed with her chest. She sat slumped over a DART tree trunk unshifting after a bee sting like a water bottle untouched yet holding strong during a downpour. She ripped apart her fingers flinging flesh like sticks before a tent setup. She tossed and turned on her air mattress like being lullabied to dyke orgasms before suffocation. She curled up in the ferns like they were blankets during the dew of night stage. She walked around with her sister, eating Vag-onuts like they were her last meal. She cried butch-bottled tears in Oasis like she was being anointed into the sisterhood of sensitivity she could never have imagined. She taps her inked up shoulder in the food line for Moroccan stew like she was a healer. She says, "I am glad you are here, sister," and I smiled, recharged, and reflected "I am here, she is not, and I am enough."

2015

This was it. It was when she was here with me. I slide my hand under her shirt, caressing her warm body in the cold field. Her head is back, back arched, lips half bit off. She remembers her promise, "next year I will be there fucking you under the stars." She is now there under the stars with me, except I am fucking her. I gaze into her glimmering eyes, grab her black, nail polished, little fingers, and lead her back to the woods behind night stage. I lean her against a tree, peel off her tight jeans, and devour her, feeling her hand pull my hair. She moans, squirts back at me, and then I fist her. I imagine the bark inking up the small curve of her back, her long, dark hair wrapping around it like a halo, and her arms extending up through the branches like she was holding onto the Big Dipper's swing. I look up to see her raised cheek, smile-kiss her long and hard, and together we rise up, hearts shooting like Falcon River's flaming arrows and LV's fireworks from her stashed canon, like white-fire stars, after Hanifah Walidah.

***

It was the moment when the sun fades, the wind blows, and the dragonflies buzz before the lights stream rainbows. I put on my hoodie, grab the pipe, invite my girl to my chest, and stretch out on the blanket in the Chem Space one last time during the final Saturday night stage. I swallow the smoke hard and breathe in crisp air. I am excited for the start of the performance, but unable to process the end of the festival. The moment comes, "hello, sisters," Elvira Kurt screams, and then later, "damn you, Lisa Vogel." My heart does cartwheels and then collapses into the soil. Chix Lix keeps us rocking hard late into the night to the beats many of us dream would have been blasting at our dyke proms and feminist protests, but as a writer and academic, I am struck by the linear timeline of political rhetoric and herstorical shout-outs to the radical womyn shape- shifters—Emma Goldman, Assata Shakur, Annie Mae Aquash, and Gloria Steinem, among our numerous other foremothers who have made this life more livable for us younger sisters receiving the torches. I am in the most radical time warp of my life, and yet I am thinking about Lisa Vogel. I think about presence and absence. LV, presente? I also am wondering about the womyn who have been attending all 40. Amazons, presente? I am 35, I have attended for 5 consecutive years, and I am wondering how I will survive, too. How will we all survive in the hetero-patriarchy, where we never were meant to survive? Are we just herstory now? Where do we go from here? What else is there? As Mayor Toshi proclaims, are we "there and back again?" I am here, not there, not anywhere, but there everywhere. I remember Gina Breedlove's last tune and LV's last words at closing ceremony, I remember sisters using their hands to put out the flame, and yet I still feel the fire on my fingertips, where the opening night's chalk has not settled.

2016

I desire tractors going through the woods, functioning as headlights to the Zone. I desire dragonflies, landing on my arms when a sister shares peace cranes. I desire words off the page, like badass, topless womyn in the sun.

I desire kisses in front of Janes, stopping only to smile and remember your self in her. I desire head-bobs in the tent, listening to womyn chant "we shall overcome." I desire labryses on womyn's necks, cutting through the ripest watermelons. I desire lanterns in the darkest eve, lighting the way towards the Amazonian Revolution. I desire the Land's soil in my hands, cupped yet falling into the 40th Fest mug, from which my lips will never part.

## Shall Never Be

I.

who are (you)? (i) am no-body. (i) am not some-body. (i) don't exist. (you) do not exist. (we) do not exist. characters are symbols. nations are imagi(nations). planets are plutos. nothing exists. being is not thinking. becoming is not breathing. matter does not matter. atoms are phantoms. illusions are delusions.

II.

who aren't you? i am not a human. i am a social text. i am a body of knowledge. i am a category. i am a margin. i am, because i am not. i am trans. I am nonbinary. i am white (trash). i am queer. i am unamerikan. i mean, because i mean less. i am somebody, because i am nobody. I am unfree.

# (S)election Night

*(for Flavia Rando)*

I was at the Lesbian Herstory Archives on election eve. I peed with Gertrude Stein hovering over me. I sat around a table of lesbians and queers drinking a dozen kinds of teas, with our fierce Radicalesbian leader, artist, archivist, commune rice cooker, and retired art history professor Flavia Rando encouraging us to "use our political imagination" while coughing up dust, foreshadowing the disgust of the next day. We talked about our lives and theories—the personal and the political—until queer bed time, oftentimes summoned by a bathroom break, a yawn, or some synched up fidgets. I talked about grassroots resistance, silently scoffing and rolling my eyes at the anxiety folks communicated about Trump. I laughed at the jokes about fascism shared by our Gay Liberation Front's Christopher Street poster dyke writer and artist, Fran Winant, who reminds us to "eat rice and have faith in women." I did not think it would happen. I went to a feminist friend's apartment nearby to continue the chuckles over drinks. We all made a Trump dart board with removable hair, blasted and danced to a satire of "Total Eclipse of the Heart" with her dog, talked about mansplainers, ate vegan pizza and cookies, and checked in every hour or so for an update, knowing it was just a pretense to shoot the shit, throw down, smoke a fat one, and chill out. After a couple of hours, however, despite Clinton winning the popular vote, it took a bleak turn, with Trump "winning" states. We flipped through the channels, realizing it was not a surreal Octavia Butler dystopian novel, that the world has gone to shit, but indeed, a reality check confirmed by an Italian friend at 4AM, "sorry about your country, mate." Waking up to this text next to my subversive cats, I realized we were not just living under capitalism, but a nascent totalitarian state.

# Flowers with a Side of Vodka

*(for Cheryl Clarke)*

I remember the first time I read Cheryl Clarke almost two decades ago. I was just getting into Women's, Gender, and Sexuality Studies, reading tons of feminist theory and critiques of racism and homophobia within the women's movement. I picked up *This Bridge Called My Back*, and read "Lesbianism: An Act of Resistance." I was coming out as a baby dyke, and had little understanding of sexual orientation as a personal identity, let alone as a political identity. I never thought I would be queer—and later trans—but her early work deeply influenced my awakening as a writer, as an activist, as a scholar, and as a radical queer and trans feminist. I continued to her Black feminist theoretical work in *Home Girls*. I appreciate her work on women like Audre Lorde and Nikki Giovanni in the Black Arts Movement. I moved onto her poetry. I fell in love with Althea and Flaxie and the rest of *Living as a Lesbian*. It is some my favorite butch/ femme writing to this day. Her poetic voice is raw, subversive, vivid, and aesthetically beautiful. I was overjoyed it was republished, and I could teach it the first time I taught LGBTQ Literature—not to mention include Clarke's work in my Women and Literature class and always in my Feminist Theory and Queer Theory classes. I watched her all butched out as June in *The Watermelon Woman,* and recently saw her with Faye reunited again at the Lohman. I smiled as I heard her say she also read Clarke as a baby dyke and dreamed of being with her then. I admired her poetic and scholarly work. I never thought I would get the privilege of getting to know Clarke as a person, though. She edited my article on Pat Parker for the *Journal of Lesbian Studies*, and I never laughed so hard at a reviewer's comments for a revise and resubmit. She writes in the margins, "I feel like a bad dyke, but say more about her ex-husbands and violence here." In addition, I met her two summers ago at Women Writers in Bloom, and listened to her read her new poetry. I don't go to the Bronx from Brooklyn for anyone, but it was worth it to hear new poems from her book *By My Precise Haircut.* I was intrigued by the form of the workshop, her slipping papers to us with sentences and asking us to write about them, as well as hearing her read poems ranging in theme from slaves to deer. She signed my book, "Red, I'll edit you anytime. Write on." And she did. She invited me to her Hobart Women Writers conference. I attended with a friend. Clarke, blocking traffic in an orange shirt, greeted us, yelling "Red Washburn" across the street and told where to park. I did some of my best summer writing in the Catskills there during the workshop on *duende* in which she was a participant, and loved hearing her feedback on my creative writing; she generously offered and later moved onto gentrification and resistance over lunch. It was a solid combo of politics and poetry for me with the gorgeous mountains and kind folks by the fire. I never thought I would leave there and get an email from her inviting me to hang with her and her dog, listen to her stories about some of my favorite writers—such as Leslie Feinberg, Minnie Bruce Pratt, Audre Lorde, and Michelle Cliff, and her poem reflections on her lesbian Suburu— and discuss writing a book on political writing. She is one of the only badasses to whom I will give flowers with a side of vodka.

# Cliff Notes: On Identity, Memory, and Community

*(for Michelle Cliff)*

—

I am remembering how I learned history. Memorize this fact. Know this date. Know this president. Know this war. Know this map. Know this concept. Know this tactic. Know this rhetoric. Know all these boring details, but do not know structural power. Michelle Cliff writes, "How do we capture the history that remains only to be imagined?" This question begs us to inquire about knowledge and power as connected to "fictive history."

—

What is history? I remember in sixth grade the teacher spoke about the founding fathers. He read off of antiquated notes, yellowed like his smoke-reeking fingers. He insisted they left England on a quest for life, liberty, and the pursuit of happiness. They won the American Revolution, fighting for and establishing a new nation that promoted democracy and equality. They penned the Constitution, to which citizens were accountable. There was justice for all.

—

Whose history? I remember in college the professor spoke about the fathers differently, as unfounders. She pounded the podium with her fist, reverberating off chalkboards like chants in bullhorns. She offered a historical corrective: they left England because they did not want to pay British taxes, stole land from Native Americans, enslaved them and Black people, raped women, slaughtered children, and pillaged those communities with their smallpox blankets. They wrote their treaties to preserve their wealth and power. There was no justice for all.

—

What is struggle? I remember in grad school the professor spoke about history as a site of resistance. She asked us to pop a hole in a piece of paper, look through it, and see another angle of vision. She showed us how small actions matter in numbers. Marginalized people revolted, wanting the right to be free, to exist, to live, to be. They took to the streets, advocating for civil rights, women's rights, indigenous rights, LGBTQ rights, among others. They marched on Washington, defended themselves at Stonewall, protected Pine Ridge, protested the Miss America Pageant, and organized sits in at Woolsworth's, among others. They got the right to vote, to have abortions, to get divorced, to work, to get housing, to get food, to not be harassed. They wanted freedom and liberation for all.

—

Whose voice? I remember all the subversive women, gender nonconforming, genderqueer, nonbinary, and trans folks, and queer writers, artists, historians, and theorists I have gotten my hands on for various feminist knowledge projects the last fifteen years as a scholar, writer, and professor. Shout out to Virginia Woolf, Assata Shakur, Emma Donoghue, Gloria Anzaldua, Monique Wittig, Cherrie Moraga, Mary Dorcey, Ailbhe Smyth, June Jordan, Judith Butler, Jack Halberstam, Leslie Feinberg, Marsha P. Johnson, Sylvia Rivera, Joan Nestle, and Michelle Cliff, among many others. I read their stories, their testimonies, and their voices, as well as assigned them to my students. The way people remember their ancestors and represent themselves is a form of cultural citizenship and radical truth-telling in a world that expects silence as compliance.

—

I am challenging how I learned history. I have learned from many radical thinkers how to evaluate knowledge through the spectrum of difference and power. As Elsa Barkley Brown says, "History is everybody talking at once, multiple rhythms being played simultaneously. The events and people we write about did not occur in isolation but in dialogue with a myriad of other people and events. [. . .] As historians we try to isolate one conversation and to explore it, but the trick is then how to put that conversation in a context which makes evident its dialogue with so many others." As Joan Nestle states, "To live without history is like to live like an infant, constantly amazed and challenged by a strange and unnamed world. There is a deep wonder in this kind of existence, a vitality of curiosity and a sense of adventure that we do well to keep alive all of our lives. [. . .] To live with history is to have a memory not just of our lives but the lives of others, people we have never met but whose voices and actions connect to our collective selves. [. . .] Because of the work of grassroots national and international lesbian and gay historians, we have found patterns both in our oppression and in our responses. We can begin to analyze what went wrong and what went right. [. . .] History makes us, at one and the same time, part of a community and alone as we watch the changes come. [. . .] Living with history maybe burdensome, but the alternative is exile. We would never have the chance to embrace each other, to urge each other on and telling the whole story. [. . .] The choices we make based on these voices and our own lives is the living gift we bequeath to our lesbian daughters. Every present becomes the past, but caring enough to listen will keep us all alive." Angela Davis remarks, "We are thankful for the legacies, but we do not receive them uncritically." Taken together, I hear the echoes of these women's and trans voices as I create my own critical voice. I have been thinking about the dialogues we have across time and space, those with and between intergenerational dykes, queers, gender nonconforming, nonbinary, genderqueer, and trans folks in diverse communities, both as unliving and living herstory and theirstory. Herstory and theirstory are nonlinear, memory is asymmetrical, and testimony is an ongoing feminist trans project, but how do we create a world that bridges then and now and where we are traveling on our own without a colonial and white supremacist map?

—

I am learning my herstory and theirstory. As Michelle Cliff writes, "I am untangling the filaments of my history." I remember reading and taking notes on Cliff in grad school, first in Contemporary Women's Autobiography, second in Postcolonial Literature and Theory, third in Caribbean Literature, fourth in my own undergrad class Sexuality and Literature, and lastly in Lez Create: Dyke Arts Workshop this summer, just after her death, the day of the Pulse shootings. We sat around the table at the Lesbian Herstory Archives with its numerous queer feminist spirits. We propped our heads up, pushed up our ears, flipped pages in books, and stared at signs that read "sisterhood feels good" and see a painting of two women's nipples touching, as we read our ancestors who have passed on recently—Audre Lorde, Adrienne Rich, Leslie Feinberg, Jeanne Cordova, and Michelle Cliff, among others. "This is their headquarters; where they write history. Around tables they exchange facts—details of the unwritten past. Like the women who came before them—the women they are restoring to their work/ space—the historians are skilled at unraveling lies; are adept at detecting the reality beneath the erasure," Michelle Cliff writes in "Against Granite." We pulled *Claiming an Identity They Taught Me to Despise* off the shelf, read "Passing," exchanged feedback on systems of discrimination—racism, sexism, classism, heterosexism, and colonialism—listened to her read "Notes on Speechlessness," and used a writing prompt on gender, power, and difference. We read her back alive and gave ourselves permission to be. We listen to her words in our own voices. We hear her legacy and speak back to her with authority. We have our own identity and authenticity, but she is part of our ancestry and community. She was one of our trailblazers, but we are the shapeshifters now. "The historians—like those who came before them—mean to survive," Cliff still whispers to her sisters and other siblings through her writing.

—

What is herstory now? I remember Nancy Bereano's Firebrand and Phase 1's *The L Word* screenings and annual Phasefests. I even remember Ginger's as dyke and trans-friendly exclusive, before cis and straight people and cis and gay men co-opted it. I even remember Bluestockings when it carried *Sinister Wisdom*, before the entire journal was written off as transphobic, including me as an out genderqueer, nonbinary, trans, and gender non-conforming contributor to it, by the same circles who label the entire second-wave as transphobic. I even remember Women's, Gender, and Sexuality Studies programs and dyke marches when there were no cis straight or gay men in them. I remember the Michigan Womyn's Music Festival from the butch struts to the trans allies in understanding workshops—the hopes and the blocks. I remember archiving it. I remember editing a book about it. I still remember my writing about it. I remember the feeling of being there. I still find places and spaces where lesbian/ queer feminist culture is honored—Sisterspace, People Called Women, the Lesbian Herstory Archives, Otherwild, the NYC Dyke March, Henrietta Hudson, the Hobart Women Writers Festival, Women in Bloom, Million Women Drummers, *Sinister Wisdom*, and Women's, Gender, and Sexuality Studies conferences, programs, and events, among others. However, power and privilege, coupled with rampant misogyny and ageism, has created the erasure of many lesbian feminist separatist spaces. I worry deeply about the survival of the remaining ones in queer, gay, and trans communities, and I also worry deeply about egregious transmisogyny and transphobia in some lesbian feminist spaces. I worry about the consequences of struggle without solidarity—the alternative to our alternatives—that maintain the hegemonic power structure within which marginalized communities are trying to live and trying to survive.

—

What is the future of herstory, theirstory, and other stories? I neither want to think about lesbian herstory as a mere past, nor that and the queer and trans future just as a contentious and/or inaccurate archive. I want to honor the unliving herstory, to engage with both living herstory and theirstory, and to create intergenerational spaces in which feminism, anti-racism, and anti-colonialism are centered and pluralized. I want to preserve and celebrate our collective inheritance and refine and re-create the present and the future by designing and promoting autonomous zones that center lesbian/ queer feminist experiences and realities, but also are safe and welcoming to people who exist outside of gender and sexual binaries—trans folks across the spectrum, FTMs, MTFs, agenders, bigenders, genderfucking folks, gender outlaws, transbutches, genderqueers, nonbinary folks, and other gender-nonconforming folks, etc.— and these spaces not to be dominated by white folks. I toggle in between these spaces as someone who straddles both the political category of butch, nonbinary, and transmasculine and also personal identities of queer—the personal is still political. I do not want to live in a world where someone cannot respect the language or leadership of women anymore than someone who cannot respect the language or solidarity of someone outside the binary system. They are both feminist issues within lesbian and queer spaces, and we are losing them due to horizontal hostility in ways gay men and trans people are getting more access and visibility. I want a world that transforms the possibilities between lesbian and queer spaces for women and trans folks across the spectrum.

—

I imagine a world where the "'L' does not disappear," as Bonnie Morris puts it. A world where the "Q" does not dominate in ways "G" still does. Where "women" is not removed from Women's, Gender, and Sexuality Studies. Where "T" represents more than FTM and MTF and the spectrum of gender and difference. Where "lesbian" is not footnoted in Queer Studies. I imagine a world where our language and communities share, work, and grow together in solidarity yet can build solidarities across difference with old, new, and emerging words and identities in time. I imagine cultures of resistance of history then, herstory, then and now, theirstory, here and now, herstories, theirstories, and other possible stories then and there.

III.

# St. Colleen

*(for Colleen Washburn)*

She left her mail unopened for months at a time. She got blankets, keychains, dreamcatchers, calendars, address labels, and stickers from more than a dozen charities and organizations. She did not tell anyone. She did these donations in others' names. She was a giver. She gave strangers on social media medical advice. She even helped an elderly woman on the Joan Jett fan site, a former sex worker and punk rocker, who had no one and two red legs. She gave patients her breaks, her back and neck while lifting them, and did double shifts on no sleep. She wanted to help people. She went with a cousin to gyno appointment before her own cardiologist appointment. She waited for her family to eat first. She gave her kids the last piece of bread and tissue. She gave homeless people money she did not have. She took care of others. She listened to sob stories and held out her hand. She was a listener. She was kind and gentle in her own quiet. She never said anything bad about anyone, even when they deserved it. She bit her tongue at mean people. She forgave them. She survived. She put out her hand in between fights at the dinner table. She did not like water guns. She wanted peace. She was a martyr. She put others first until the end. She deserved much better in life, her own needs met as well as a return to her caregiving, but death was quick and kind to her. What does it look like to care for a mother gone? I write to care for her, unopened, her in memory.

# When It Gets Colder

In the early morning hours before I heard my mother died, I dreamt she was already dead. I was trying to find big purple flowers in Brooklyn for her with an old friend. We walked miles and miles up and down Broadway and beyond in Bed Stuy, hitting stores, parks, and gardens. What were they? Allium, Hydrangea, or Lilacs? It is fall now. Maybe they were smaller. Asters or Irises? I was never good with classifications. Something else, something real or imaginary? Something special for her. I would keep looking for the right ones. For them all. For her. I would swipe them from neighbors up and down the lake where we lived, stuff them under my shirt, bike home, and hand them to her before she went to work at night. I would snatch her a daisy as if it was a half dollar just to see her smile. It ended in a fog. I woke up covered in tears to my partner's warm body around me. I shared the dream with her, cried some more, and drifted back off to sleep for a few hours. I knew I would see her when it got colder. That was what she wanted. I texted her the night before to visit. It was fall now. Suddenly. I woke up again to my cat purring loudly beside me, just minutes before the call. The home phone. I knew. I picked up. I watered them all. Hard. It happened a few hours before. My father said a single daisy bloomed in their yard, that she was at peace. He had irises out to plant. I bought daisies, irises, and an assortment of unknown purples for her grave. I could never steal enough flowers for her.

# Yesterday

She loved music, especially folk, rock, and traditional Irish. She was in bands, folks groups, and choirs, particularly involved in St. Joseph's in New Windsor and Sacred Heart in Newburgh, where she could combine her musical and religious interests with her husband and her numerous friends. She was an extraordinary singer and skilled guitar player. I remember the beauty and power of her voice. It would flutter through the house like a bird on a porch, inviting us to look at the life there. She would smile and lift us up with her magic, whether she was cooking us Mac 'N Cheese with chicken nuggets, brushing our hair before school, driving to the store with her wet, Suave-washed hair outside the sunroof, practicing songs with the church folk group over Irish coffee, pigs in a blanket, Doritos, and baked ziti, or enjoying concerts with her mother and kids, including Joan Jett, Joan Baez, Ringo Starr, U2, James Taylor, Carole King, Joni Mitchell, The Who, Green Day, Cherish the Ladies, Celtic Woman, and the Duprees, among many others, with her always leaving with a souvenir cup. In particular, I remember how alive she was singing the Beatles, whom she adored since she was a teen, even seeing *A Hard Day's Night* with her cousin and little sister. She knew all the words to them all, "Yesterday," "Let It Be," "PS I Love You," etc., and while singing such dulcet tunes, she would get her body hard into it, tapping her foot and bobbing her head. She laughed when I would sing Beatles songs to my cats Lux and Volt and insert their names in them, "Luxie in the Sky with Diamonds" and "Hey, Volt. Don't make it bad." The last concert I saw with her was Ringo Starr at Bethel Woods, one of her favorite concert venues, and I adored how much our time together and music brought her such happiness, even though she would get mad at me for trying to get her the most accessible seat, the pretzel with the most salt on it, and arrange to get the car as close to possible to her to make her life easier. I also think about how softly she would strum her guitar while singing when she played with my father, sister, and I with all the animals and my grandmother crowding around her good vibes. I think about how patient and supportive she was when I was learning guitar, first playing Simon and Garfunkel's "Feeling Groovy" on repeat, and then Green Day's "Basket Case" on electric guitar, reverberating through the house at all hours for my punk band, the Locals, and shows, the latter of which she would attend and enjoy from the back in order for me to be cool. I think about her voice every day while I walk listening to music, trying to look up, listen, and imagine it carrying over the mountains.

# Daisy

She loved animals. She had many pet kids over the years, including Toto, Bumpkin, Daisy, Hepzebah, Clotilda, Samson, and Delilah. She also had many fur grandkids, including Luxemburg, Mielziner, Voltairie, Ziggy, Onyx, Maeve, Gigi, Sadie, and Sheldon. Of all them—whether named post-seminary life by my dad, after anarchist and socialist feminists by me, or after more Irish and socially acceptable American names by my sister—my mom shared a special relationship with Daisy, named after her favorite flower. Daisy was her baby, Mama's girl. I would proclaim "Mama's home" to Daisy, and she would howl, run around, and greet her at the door in the morning. She would sleep with her. Daisy and my mom would watch TV together, mainly *ER*, *Grey's Anatomy*, *Titanic*, *Sister Act*, *Dirty Dancing*, and PBS and Hallmark movies. In particular, I remember how adorable it was when Daisy would howl the intro to *General Hospital*. I remember how much it made my mom smile and laugh. For Daisy, that song signified the joy of uninterrupted hour with her, a chance at a cheese sandwich, and her side of diet Wild Cherry Pepsi soda. She would snuggle on the couch with Daisy's head on her tired legs. That was their time. Until the end, she spoiled her, feeding her cookies as she was dying, just as the shelter did when her hips gave out before we adopted her. It was the sweetness there I learned and cherished in my own special bonds with animals, especially Heps and Lux. I adored how much my mom loved my cats, especially Lux. She would pick up him up, pet and kiss him, and laugh at his Industrial Revolution purr. When Lux visited, my mom would keep the door open for him to go outside and drink his lemonade under the bush, deliver him food and treats, and ask in her high-pitched voice, "hey, how's my grandson?" with him meowing back in his soft, sweet voice. She also would laugh at my stories of Lux greeting me at the door, with his robe, slippers, and hot chocolate after visiting her upstate with him staying in the city, not driving with his lead foot and paying all the tolls on my lap. She loved hearing about Lux's outdoor adventures, health struggles with arthritis and diabetes, and how my sidekick took care of me when I was down and sick. She would be happy to know that Lux sat beside me as I wrote this piece as well as during my hardest cries after she died. Volt sat beside me, too, in between thinking about bird murder. I can see Daisy back in her arms now.

# Mother Teresa's Stethoscope

I see her in all of them. The nurses. The ones walking around PACU. The RNs. The ones with white smocks, then later stylish blue, purple, and flower smocks. They watch me. A gentle touch, pulse check. A caring grin, a temperature read. A funny story, a pill delivery. They see me waking up. Strangers in/with hospital wings, they keep me up. I hear her in all of them. Their medical assessment. A barf bag. A water pitcher. A pain reliever. A wheelchair. Their kind monitoring. A shuffle step. I think about how well she took care of others, bandaging cousins' boo-boos as a kid to filling IV bags to listening to recovering hearts as an adult, her feet heavy, almost five decades of her eyes baggy, her neck spasming. I still feel her here with me. In a MRI, I listen to her. I hear her breathing in the stethoscope on me. The sound of a smile from heaven.

# Pink Shaving

I asked her if she needed anything. She always said "no," but this time she wanted a razor. She has not showered in a month, does not brush her hair, and only gets dressed in her street clothes when they make her go to physical therapy and community meals during the day, but she wanted a shave. I placed the pink razor next to her, and she pointed to her face. I asked her if needed help. She did. She wanted me to shave her moustache. I lathed her up, went from side to side, up and down, and went slowly. I thought about how I never knew the right way. I watched my father in front of the mirror growing up. I have shaved everyday since I was thirteen, the gift of PCOS. I have been growing out my natural beard for almost a year. I stood over her in her gown, her beardless. I was gentle with her. She needed and deserved that. There was no razor burn.

# Let It Be

*

She rocked her leg horizontally while sitting.

*

She re-watched "nobody puts Baby in the corner."

*

She made railroad tracks in her Mexican food plate.

*

She headbanged and yeah-ed after a three-pointer.

*

She brought her bowling ball luggage purse to physical therapy.

*

She read Danielle Steel and Mary Higgins Clark on the toilet with a cig.

*

She liked black and white cookies and peanut butter, not together.

*

She had a wedgie since she gave birth to me.

*

Her mottos were "I'm doing the best I can," "Be nice," and "That's different."

*

She loved to talk about the Pope being less homophobic with time.

*

She had change purses from other countries.

*

She rocked trivia and crossword puzzles.

*

She had nine toes in the end.

*

She was hot in short sleeves, even in the winter.

*

She shuffle-stepped in white rockers and slip ons.

*

She gave the best medical advice and had a medicine cabinet you'd get sick for.

*

She showed up and helped all, whether loved ones or strangers.

*

She left her baby powder on the bathroom floor.

She had cozy nightgowns and fleece sweatshirts.

Her nails were good picks, her voice was a good earworm.

She collected Bethel Woods and WNBA souvenir cups.

She was never right after her mom died, no one is.

She voted for Hilliary Clinton by the lake.

She read *People*, AARP, and a bunch of mags about cats and health.

She accepted help with the trash, snow shoveling, and bringing in groceries.

Her favorite coffee cup had a goose on it.

She wore hippie blouses with black stretch waist pants covered in cat/dog hair.

She was all about Claddagh rings, scrunchies, and barrettes.

Her favorite food was diner burgers and pork fried rice.

She wore Chantilly perfume, curled her hair, and put on blue eye shadow to dress up.

She would taste test her light and sweet coffee and hold up the line without caring.

She sent sappy and cheesy Hallmark cards to her kids for every holiday and just because.

She got drunk with her kids in a dragon canoe in Baltimore.

She went to Ireland and tolerated my castle excursions and curry breath.

She would not let me get a water gun as a kid because she was a pacifist.

She played mini golf with us in wrist splints.

*

She wore #1 Mom necklaces from school fairs with pride.
*

She loved parades, fireworks, and rock concerts with her kids and mom.
*

She chilled by the community pool and on the house porch with her mom.
*

She was always up on the latest beats.
*

She liked the Jersey shore, especially Wildwood, and played in arcades with us.
*

She named her "get well" stuffed animal cat present Princess.
*

She didn't get to see Trump lose.
*

Our last conversation was about RBG.
*

I wish I could have opened more doors for her.

# Cardinal Payphone

She was the first person I called. When I got a job. Got a ticket. Got a scholarship. A PhD. A girlfriend. Divorced. A cat. Was sick. Was high. Tenure. A book deal. The first person I called. Anything good. Anything bad. Just to say hi. My mom. My first, best, and longest friend. Like my Nan was to her. My mom. I listen to her missed calls. Her message on her landline. Her voice. It still comforts me. I think about calling her cell. Who has her number now? I look for her out there. A rabbit eating grass. A cardinal eating seeds. A squirrel eating a mushroom. A bluejay chasing a junco. I send her a note down a creek. I pull out a chin hair and blow her a wish off a mountain. I watched the leaves reach their peak. After she died. Time is before and after she died now. After she died. The leaves blew off the tree by her grave. I close my eyes. I feel her as they fall. I breathe. How do we communicate with the dead? Catch the leaves—how humans give hugs to the dead.

# Wake Me up When September Ends

It has been two months since she died. It's been three months since I started T. It's been eight months living on lockdown with my family upstate. It's been seven months since my first born cat was diagnosed with diabetes. It's been eight months teaching fully online. I'm two weeks away from hysto/oopho. Many parts of me have transitioned since her heart gave out.

—-

The day she died I learned how hard it was to chew toast, to take a walk without loosing my footing, to get shot up with vitamin T and not feel, to sleep without picturing her eyes and mouth open on her chair.

—

On (S)Election Day and Halloween, Biden and trick-or-treaters, I didn't call the home line just to hear her voice. On Thankstaking, I called, and I heard it. I thought about bringing her a coconut custard pie. I stood there cutting potatoes and cried into them.

—

I walked into Walmart for a ring light. I saw her fleece sweatshirts, her Wild Cherry Diet Pepsi, and her Tidy Cat litter. I would not find her in those aisles. I couldn't cry, much less breathe. All there was was panic and void.

—

I listen to the Beatles on walks. "Yesterday," "Let it Be," "Help," I know all the words, the way she tapped her foot, bobbed her head, the way she laughed when I sang the songs to my cats with their names in them, "Luxie in the Sky with Diamonds" and "Hey, Volt. Don't make it bad." I think about her hair outside her sunroof, belting out the lyrics and her voice carrying over the mountains.

—-

It's a pandemic. It's lockdown. Nothing feels real out there. I had to see her body to believe she was blue. I hurt everywhere. I can't read a novel. I can't follow a routine. I don't have a compass. I don't feel safe. I don't sleep, and I am beyond tired. But I do still think she's alive sometimes, then I feel it. The absence. That stays and never goes. A brain injury. That I carry with me. I am slow for it. She never liked to be rushed.

# In the River

I stand in the river like I did in front of her dead body. I hold my head low to the earth, with a latex glove palming her cold face, cry-staring at her, her hands around me, not sure what feels real in COVID time. I see water spewing out of my five holes where my broken ovaries, fallopian tubes, uterus, and cervix once lived like the Virgin Mary with blood dripping down her face in a Catholic school bathroom. I tilt to witness, a fountain-teapot of sorts, listening for sounds of her heart pumping hot blood out of her ventricles when she once lived. She birthed me, one ovary, c-section, her partial hysto, scars now ash. I give her what I never wanted, dysphoric offerings for the ancestors. There we end the line, connect the doctors' dots, and exit bodies no longer ours. I used to get my period when I saw her, but I won't see her or have it anymore. Parts of me left with her, a leaf released from her graveside tree now floating down the river I cannot stand in, no fish at her feet, the gift of matrilineal death. I flow there. I remember her.

# The Eulogy She Read

*(Colleen for Bernie)*

*Here, where I am capacious, alive, with pink glasses toasting to ghost statue
etchings that do not translate. We dig into the dirt on rainy, cloudy nights,
searching for ancestral portals, not graves/dreams I fear. Underneath, in it,
creativity is not sour-ed, relationships I remember like their breath.*

Mom and I always were best friends. We shared everything from blood to
bonding. We talked every day about everything—the family, work, health,
television, music, and life in general. We got lunch together at Neptune and
Union Square or Burger King or Wendy's. We went shopping together for the
best deals for diet soda at Shoprite or Stop 'N Shop or for clothes at Walmart or
Ames. We shared music interests, ranging from Mom attending my St. Joseph's
and Sacred Heart folk group gigs to treating ourselves to local oldies like the
Duprees shows. We talked health, ranging from diabetes to arthritis, with me
being her unofficial doctor. We both shared a determination to survive, a strong
work ethic, a devotion to our children and grandchildren, and a commitment
to compassion. Mom took every opportunity to brag about me. She respected,
admired, and loved me collectively more than anybody. My most salient
memory of this fact was her public acknowledgement at her retirement party
from West Point. Mom extolled me in her speech, focusing on my kindness
and thoughtfulness. Mom closed her speech by saying that we all could become
better people by learning from my example "to never say anything bad about
another person," at which my friend and fellow bandmate, sitting across from
me, nodded instinctively. My kids have learned from our relationship that your
first best friend is your mother. I have carried on this tradition with them. They
hope their pets think the same about them.

IV.

# Crestview Tree Woman

*(for Bernadette McGuire)*

We all used to go to the local lake, Crestview. We went swimming there together. At lunch time, away from the lake and just in front of the parking lot, we sat under a huge, shady Maple tree, marked with several love tattoos. We sat on her pink blanket. She sat on her blue-striped beach chair. We ate boloney and cheese sandwiches, jelly cookies, and peaches from her Styrofoam cooler. We shared many precious memories there: playing air hockey and ping-pong in the game room; getting scolded for running in the bathroom, and doing so barefoot; building castles, characterized almost exclusively by lots of tunnels, and burying us in the sand; singing "Walking in the Beach in the Hot Sand" with us, and then darting into the water with laughter; attending "tea parties" under the water, where we sat under water sipping tea; losing "beauty pageants" on the path to the water to her; her playing "motorboat" in the water with us (it was a game where she spun us in the water like a motorboat, saying "motorboat, motorboat goes so slow" and, ultimately, building to its climax, "motorboat, motorboat goes so fast"); eating Mario's cherry frozen ices (always cherry) with them; playing Black Jack and Old Maid with us for hours in the evening under her favorite shady tree at Crestview; and all of us teasing her about the fish coming after her feet, her biggest fear. She loved Crestview. It later it defined her identity. They called her the "Crestview tree woman" there. The space is now officially gone, like her—covered up and nonexistent—but it always will be place of peace for me. We came from dirt. Her roots remain. We breathe from trees. We grow with water. My Crestview Tree Woman is still here with me.

# How Do You Love a Ghost?

between sunset park and south slope,
the descent to hell begins,
the land where stones become people,
just off of 18th street between 7th and 8th ave.
greenwood.

where the raccoons roam,
where lady liberty guards,
where birds doubled-dutched the power lines,
where the wind played piñata with traffic lights,
where the clouds pissed after crossing their legs for hours,
where the stop signs are urban optionales,
where these days are always dreams deferred,
where helium heart's hovered over the hood,
where your handwriting can't comfort as much as her words,
where a brave valentine's missive traveled far from the grave.

there where her voice is trapped in my voicemail.
there where my poems become metas.
there where we have her cards.
there where we talk about you without you.
there where we miss you like bloody hell.
there where you can't communicate well.

where is the land where all the lost socks go?
is it high? is it low?
i never wanted to know.
i cupped my ears, letting your (un)forgotten face talk go,
no matter how tall i would grow.

where is the boo-boo-kisser, wound-licker, smile-grabber?
here there is dirt under the nails,
here there are sleepies in the eyes,
here there are meaningful deaths,
here there are meaningless lives,
here there everywhere just where has the flying balloonhead gone?

## What Is Felt There

the minute before
hot decaf hits
the tongue
translates the palpable
taste bud trauma
an inevitable burn
lingering like her
death.

# Macramé Keychain


she dances jigs in bounces,
shifting her weight from one foot to another,
like a jump roper during recess
pogo-balling to staccato strokes and harmonics,
donning her communion dress and combat boots,
still clutching her gun to her chest, as she would her cat,
when the music dies.

she spins around and around and around,
like a spinning top,
feeling like she rolled down a hill,
collapsing on the floor in giggles.
she makes sonar sounds,
like a dolphin,
before she stains the floorboard red.
she hears it.
she swims through the dirt and insects.
stroke after stroke
stroke after stroke
stroke after stroke
she counts in threes, one for each decade she knew her.
tears loosen her path.
she swims like a mermaid with coattails.
she hears it.

she hears the jewelry box.
she hears the keys to the treasure chest.
she knocks on the wooden coffin,
like teeth chattering.
she snugs the skeleton.
She sleeps with her,
like death is breath.

# St. Francis

in the space between
coffin
and
stone,
there is life
somewhere
above
the saint's cemetery,
like varicose veins,
stretching lavender across the sky,
her waving matter in my mind.

# Squire

thank heavens for helicopters,
pointing to propellers,
searching for breath,
they called to her.

she wanted pool power.
blue bathing caps,
skirty, high femme bathing suits,
towel robes,
big eighties sunglasses,
eyebrows drawn in, pink lipstick.

she wanted outdoor adventure.
motorboat and tea parties,
freezer bag picnics,
green jello orange soda animal crackers ripe peaches meaty sandwiches,
stories and cards,
poe, shakespeare, and irving.
handball on front door and red raspberries from butterfingers.

she wanted beauty, no matter what, and she was that
in the chlorinated/ urinated pool & brick tennis wall community,
where she lived, where we lived, where we always will live from somewhere else.

# Pretzel Cigars

Every day I wake up to soreness. I wake up to bruises and scratches. I cannot recall from where I got them. After all this time on this planet, I have not yet figured out how much space my body actually consumes, like liquid spreading out as far as it can in a given enclosed space. The results are there and real. The bruises always seem to heal—they always have, even with years of sports and their injuries—but the scabs remain until they scar on some rare occasions. Like a kid smacking her glued hands together until the dryness sets in and can be peeled off, I pick and re-pick the scabs when I am nervous, anxious, and stressed. The scabs sit on my lap now for you. You always reprimanded me for that. You told me to pick the salt off the pretzel cigars instead. We would smoke pretzel cigars with root beer floats on your kitchen stools. We avoided the poverty of oranges with peanut butter, post-domestic violence. But now I hurt from being free to do what I want with my scabs. I need some bandages stat. I look in your car. The seats still have salt all over them. The driver's side still smells like your makeup. Your sunglasses and visor are still in the glove box. The ketchup is still in your cup-holder, brown like our cycle's end. Elvis is still in the CD player. Your beach chair is still in the trunk. I sit in the car. You left it to me. You still feel here. I open your sunroof. Where did the warmth go?

## Sacred Heart

cavernous halls that narrow to the virgin mary,
not envisaged bleeding in a bathroom mirror
nor in an orange #57 cheese doodle,
and to you,
emerging eloquent and elegant,
always decorated—clip-on earrings, long skirts, colorful scarves, bleached
blonde hair—
from the gym where my tomboyed injuries occurred and
sweat sleeps, stomped
in the
floor forever, fossil-like.
i race to sis and to you in my
catholic school cardigan sweater,
wrinkled white shirt,
knee-high socks,
pig tails, and
plaid skirt
flapping with intensity,
like the pages of a bible,
forgotten,
under a tree on windy day,
so eager to embrace
the moment with you,
eating bbq hot chips, drinking chocolate milk, and talk, talk, talking to you
—free from beyond the black halled, checkered floor prison gates—
on grandparents' day at school,
before the days of blown-up condoms (in between) classes.

# Label Maker

*"You came back from the dead to watch tv? I said. [. . .] I sat with you, watching you watch it for a half an hour. Then I thought maybe I should offer you a cup of tea. But wasn't there some folklore rule about not giving the dead food, or not accepting food from them? Well, but this was you. And also, obviously, it wasn't you; this was my imagination. I could offer a figment of my imagination tea if I wanted."*
—Ali Smith, *Artful*


She had a lot of boxes, office boxes from West Point, the dental wing where she worked for decades before she died, some brown, some white, all had handles on the ends, along with the cadet insignia. They lived on the top of her two tall closets reeking of stank perfume, the doors open, forever off their tracks and unrepaired, above her gaudy purple dresses, flowery blouses, and heels she slept in that she collected from her prom to her AARP membership, not letting them go, like foil wrap, candles, batteries, buttons, and pennies. She stashed them where she could not reach them but beckoned for help religiously—"Hey, Aim, can you come give me a hand here?," not a question but some answers in there. They all were stacked two or three in a row. They were marked with black or green sharpies, masking tape and different colored pens from her coffee jar she swiped from her alienating secretarial jobs. They all had labels—white, off to white, yellowing from antiquity like a seasoned professor's lecture notes. They contained the things she collected—her decorations for Halloween/Samhein, St. Pat's, the Easter Rising, and Christmas, the holidays for which Irish Catholics like to throw down Jameson and Magners, bust out bagpipes, and shovel in potatoes and stew, her taxes, her medical records, her will, her address books, her password post it notes, her son's jail letters, her ex-lover's letters, her mother's, father's, sisters', daughter's, and grandkids' birthday cards, among others. She got a label maker later. I do not remember when she got it. It had blue sticky tape and white letters. I used to sit with it in between my legs, head down, furrowed browed often as a kid, punching in letters for her box ids and notes to her to stick whenever she wanted when it rained, when her arthritis kicked in, and when she forgot she mattered, while she hummed making pasta with gravy, store-made chicken, and green Jello. Sometimes I still smile when I think about labels and what we make of them when they fall off, and we can no longer find what we need when we need it most.

# Trolley

she awakes to tears
piggy toe prints on freckled faces with
chin hair stragglers
pulled to, getting to, all too pissy dry
done dreams
lucid like those whose lips
close around cans,
the ascent to scent.

her hands over her ears like
spaghetti can-cans strung to
doors catholic smothering
moans that remind
the disproved hypothesis
of soda can theory in pew communities, year
after fucking year.

her arms
propped up on a tree stump,
tabling the plaid picnics of
peanut butter to the black
anorexic of the forest
shadows, never to be ghosted, like
the way she sat
cross-legged, scanning
flower catalogues,
her index finger turning purple, a
mind-wrinkled kiddie widdie.

her thumb crushed under a trolley—on
Christopher St.
the village
then inhabited by the Irish, the poor, the
1930s
long before the beats, the queers, the rich war—
the thumb got damaged when it wasn't in her mouth. it
always affected her thereafter,

donkey tail, thumb resting
the after in all the typists with arthritis her
stroke face, commanding the pinky to (the)
point.
her long, slender fingers

fighting for words

she lies there, naked
winter—cry-
breathe-ing into
wet cat bellies
belly button ding dongs
cheeks
that burrow
between breasts,
naked winter—she
lies there.

she draws—
penciling in her brown eyebrows in the dirt the
vacant lot, squatted by
heroin-heads in salvation army drop-offs, alone a
corporeal comma wrapping halos
around her willow tree, atop the
grass,
the cross,
the INRI fingers
combed through corn hair
bright night moon
following the circle, singing the solo, sucking the thumb, resting the index on
the nose—
about the kleenex fights that fossilize
the brown rainbow, of death
and its discontent

V.

# Nightfall

*"[W]e must take blood—metaphorically speaking. That is, we must learn how to break the surface, find the deep dangerous place where blood flows without hurting one another, and share all we know and love in order to survive."*

—Jewelle Gomez, "Forward," *The Gilda Stories*

I never have made out in a cemetery before. I never have put my jacket down to pin someone down on a headstone while listening to cis dudes pissing in the distance, smile-laughing at it all, along with a ripped dress, a bruised tit, and a phantom chest mosquito bite. I never have had a femme ask to kiss me—let alone kiss me first—anywhere, including there. Never have heard tubas, electric guitars, and singers dancing to images of skeletons in trees there. Never have seen weird films projected across lily-less ponds. Never trees lit up in sunset colors lined with fake candles. Never have seen stilt performances in wedding dresses in front of grave stones. Never seen circus puppets and jewelry box music with bats flying above costumed folks. Never have seen women harmonizing in another language in a mausoleum with incense swirling around them. I never have seen blue clouds at nightfall reflected on someone's face. I thought I had seen it all in that cemetery being in it and even locked in it. I think about this cemetery a decade later with eyes closed, ears opened, heads rested, her skull leaning into my ribs, looking up a tree with my fingers laced in her hair, laying in some peace, a leaf in my Demon Queen love's hair, where all is not dead.

# Catskills Cabin

I am lounging on your couch in my boxers with your black blanket over me in the same spot where you were the first time I came here to see you in between the cat with four eyes and the unicorn and the deer dancing under the moon prints, with my cats smooshed on the cushions purring above me, and the fire burning into the night, as I write to you. I thought about signing the guestbook, but I love handwritten notes.

I love waking up to the trees and falling asleep with the stars here. I love the beauty and the stillness here. I love reading, writing, and hiking as if they were meditation here. I love how I can breathe slower and deeper here. I love walking by your books—noting some of the writers I have read and adore, i.e., Butler, Lakshmi Piepzna-Samarasinha, Dawn, Chin, Lorde, Winterson, Sontag, Arenas, Alexie, Bornstein, Rhys, Allende, Lee, and Galloway, etc., as well as some writers I want to read, i.e., Cheng Thom, Weeks, Shraya, Binnie, and Eckermann, etc. I love seeing your handwriting in your instructions here. I love seeing the blueberry jam and other food you made here. I love seeing the wood you chopped here. I love thinking about you writing and living DIY, hard femme-style, here.

I love thinking about being here with you. I loved spooning you naked here, my small hands in between your tits and the sighs you make in between sleeping and waking. I loved the unconscious moaning I was doing next to you in my dreams here. I loved waking up to your warm skin, your tits smothering my face, your smile bright with the sun on it, your wet before I please you, your hair on my scarred chest, your eyes rolling with my hand inside you and then fixating on my gaze, your head tilted, and your mouth open, soft and gentle noises released as you give yourself to me. I loved eating your homemade bread and strawberry jam and talking about politics and white supremacy with my stubble in the morning before one your fave hikes—Rose Hill—with you. I loved taking your pink coffee mug home with me and imagining your lipstick on it. To bruises and welts everywhere—and of course, lots of face-holding.

# 2:38/2:40

I feel you smiling at me behind your book, like your nails etched in my back, before I crack my lids. I touch your eyes, and so much opens for me. I pull you close to me, wanting our ribs lined up, your tits pressed into my scars, and our bad breath swapping consciousness. I smile when you laugh before your sweet yet creepy best dog pounces on us both. This is now my fave way to wake, along with my Littles doing your hair above us and curled at our feet, even though I want to abolish mornings.

I tell you about learning left with my sucking thumb, my belly button's chastity belt, my mom pissing on her chair, how I hate looking for shit, wrote my first poem about the Knicks, raking the road shirtless with my dad, where my first feline love is buried, where my best friend lived, that I look behind me frantically while biking—and I even eat with a fork, not giving a fuck, in front of you. I am grateful you are letting me in, that you are blowing your goth cover for me. I listen to you share your dad's cooking adventures with Tabasco, your fisting fun with stilettos, seeing your fams' middle fingers, your brother aside, learning horse anatomy and not thinking about sexism in science, getting leechy with your dog, realizing stuffing down feelings pushes out joy, and politicians who are human enough to see you are kind, smart, woke, and the world is better with your vision in it.

I cherish that I could be there to hold your hand, stroke your hair, and kiss your forehead while you got out your IUD. I love that you let me fish it out for an art project of sorts, and that you let me clean off your tea bag hairball, too. I would pop two stitches, post-top surgery, for you again, and I want your cum and blood pooled in my hands, again and again.

# Dolphin Kink Convos

Florida's brightness and warmth looked so good on you, soaking up your goth skin in February. I remember us getting there, arriving at a new place together, you dropping your bags, collapsing onto the sand, tipping my black hat to shield your face, digging your back and ass into the unraked ground in your new and sexy black and red dress, airing out your freshly polished red toe nails in the wind, flashing your smile at the waves, the gulls, and my eyes, while laying on me, fossiling your sweaty tits deep into me. I cherish our dark souls open in/ to the returning sun.

# Terrarium

I think about joy with you during this pandemic—the Cobain "you are all stupid and contagious" and Manson "no touching and avoiding people life prep" memes, Zig's burnt b-day whiskers, Lux slithering through the gate to be with us and you feeding him treats out of your hand, Volt with your makeup on and Zooming with you, the green, magic forest of the Grinch House and the beauty, wonder, and adventure there, you making me witchy, fermented veggies when I was Endo sick, bringing you tea while working, you popping zits on my Jeans Pocket, cutting your hair/undercut, talking about buying a place together, sharing popcorn with you, holding your hand during our evening constitutionals, bathing with you and watching you shave, pissing with the door open intimacy, helping you through budget cuts, a health plan for your mom, taking Zig for a Red-Venture, setting up yard work and repairs, breaking down and dropping off boxes for you, you showing me your tits during breaks, thinking about canoe investments, laying on my chest watching *Crip Camp* with you, making out with you with the beast's nips on you and delivering her to you at night, folding your panties, full moon date nights at the creek with you, and talking about beavers, foxes, and geese characters. I feel at home with you wherever we are—in the woods, under the sheets, in front of the fire, spooning our animals, behind books, and on cuddled up on the couch. These moments with our "Brady Bunch" lift me up. I look forward to our blood bath on the other side.

# VI.

# Dead Horse Bay

The slow shrink of pant legs before sun suction. The feel of sand before it crumbles under teeth. The shift of ground before feet crunch glass. The static of hair before fingers graze forearms. The warmth of breath before lips suck the neck. The drop of sweat before shirts cling to tits. The rays of sun before clouds hover over polluted waves. The second before the minute changes on clock. The shadow of the hand before the pen touches the page. The flame of the sun before the glade of moon.

## Skull Sisters

The smell of swag-ash
filling the tree-line
like cunt-drenched clubs

They sat under the lunar eclipse
beating their bare chests
like skull sisters

Then they spoke in one-up tongues
chanting "rebel us" spells
like head-back moans

They rose in covert covens
stomping the system
like cigs in the dirt

They read the braceleted clouds
fingering swirl-whirl woo-woos
like witch-bitch free-mas(s)ons

And they rode the scented smoke
hanging hair-strands ablaze
like not coming up for air.

The taste of free fall
blowing "ruska" like
bubble-hearts

## 205 West End of Something

The tan carpet and unsmudged mirrors terrify almost as much as the ostentatious pearls and unwrinkled suits. I kick up my rugged Tims on the coffee table and peel off my leather jacket. I try to read more about Le's butterflies finding freedom, post-glass life. Instead, I drift to her velvet. The elevator descends to the maze of the basement, the lights dim, the walls drip burgundy. I snake through the abandoned halls to release the toxins. I head back up to the fanned top. I wait for her head check's end, one two, one two. My eye is still twitching fast like geese flying in the fog, groggy from the lack of sleep against which cats rebel unapologetically. I relax on the couch I want to stain with period blood. I think about the paint in her hair. It streaks highlights unrecognized there, a new blue that could be splashed anywhere in just the right light. The coloring shines through like the brown bracelet she wears as the warrior before her, tarnished yet polished anew.

# Mad Girl's Love Song, Part II

*Extra Jelly, Please*

I worked at D&D upstate as a teen, pouring mop bucket water into Coolata machines, putting floor-fallen everything bagels into bins, and wrapping up red-haired presents in bacon, egg, and cheese croissants for surly customers. I smoked American Spirit fags for breaks and deconstructed *Maximum Rocknroll* with my punk bassist during them before tossing in my less than two-week worn, coffee-reeking tee. Bored and alienated, wanting entertainment and compensation, we blasted the Ramones' three chords, ate lots of jelly donuts, and chucked them at each other. We rejoiced in the splat they made against us and the walls. The post-fight clean ups were worth it for the sweet times.

I stared at the drive thru menu yesterday with you. I ooze with new memories of you there—legs kicked up on the dash, sunken down in the seat with your Brooklyn hat, '70s leather jacket, green writing hoodie, and punk rock kicks— sharing your love of jelly donuts. I squirm now at your flirty pinches. I raise my dimps now at your big hold-back smiles. I pine now at your urgent head-grabs for kisses in between order and payment. I pull away with the taste of you and them in my queer vegan mouth.

*Honoring This Raw*

I got my brown Donegal Tweed Newboy cap in *Éire*, bumming around the streets of Dublin with my sister, re-visiting the old post office setting for the 1916 Easter Rising, and pub-crawling for Guinnesses and good craic along the way. We needed nomadic moments away from the political art, Republican activism, and feminist archives needed for my dissertation in the North, as well as adventurous moments with urban culture, indie entertainment, and the hustle and bustle in the South. After I purchased my cap, the only people to throw it atop their heads were my sister, who tried it on after me, and a James Joyce mime, who grabbed it to get my attention on the street. It has not had much of a life off my skull.

I melt at the picture I took of you wearing it. We swapped hats—Irish wool cap and Brooklyn baseball hat—like glasses, exchanging thoughts like visions. We dropped knowledge, such as memory as testimony, consciousness as opposition, cultural production as political contestation, narration as fiction, and lived reality and bottom-up history. We warped time like students becoming professors, reminded that academic perspective changes with object positions, desks and degrees. I tip my hat at the conversations between our brains, even if we get parking tickets during them.

*Hands on Anthropology*

I dig sociological experiments: facing the back of an elevator, pissing in the men's bathroom, sitting in a student's desk on the first day of class, yawning on the train and then counting my nearby passenger victims, and holding hands with hard femmes on the street. I uphold the authority of experience. I violate assumptions and norms. I monitor social response and public opinion. I examine the ways in which historical processes and sociological constructions of (cis)gender and (hetero)sexuality are enforced and resisted in the public sphere across a range of privileged and marginalized identities and behaviors. In particular, I view public displays of affection as both romantic affirmation and queer visibility. Criticism travels from page to stage.

I walk past Anthropologie, the store not the discipline, with you, our fingers laced. We observe the nods, smiles, look-aways, and stares. We compare seasoned yellow and immaculately white notes, voicing right-on's and fuck-you's. I feel the conflict of interest as a participant observer in love. I feel like high-fiving the allies. I feel like sheltering you from the haters. We feel better than fine.

*Stop Short, Ginger Ale Needed*

We both like to drive. I speed uncontrollably, slam on the breaks, cut off people, nose in at tolls, leapfrog in traffic, and honk at bad drivers. You drive like a lunatic, too, yet call shotty sometimes and demand ginger ale shortly after I stop short. But I will stroke your long, black hair, caress the small of your back, put my small hands in your marsupial hoodie pouch, and sing baby, "you can sleep (on my chest) while I drive," even if I almost plow through a red light doing so.

# The Sushi Verses

1
there is no "one." all is even with her, in twos.
2
a cheek bite is better than a first kiss.
3
cuddling is a good way to break bones.
4
apple granola bars for all.
5
saint anthony should not be filmed.
6
nothing says uhaul material like being cut off and flipped off.
7
ted and ken are now bound.
8
xx becomes xo, long goodbyes and frequent hellos.
9
the lower body is a comfy chair for eating scooped bagels.
10
bathrooms are for crossed legs and candy crush.
11
"mad girl's love song" contains multiples.
12
bun n' burger is beyond cheesy.
13
grown women can get ink.
14
heard from the professor's podium, is anybody sweating?
15
she lives where bendy straws and stuffed animals are valued.
16
i want your words (and fists) in me.
17
hum up holes, breathe me.
18
"the yellow wallpaper[ed]" rooms have visiting hours.
19
an emo badass is always a pleasure.

20
the last cup was not in a to-go cup.
21
"i miss you" comes within minutes after departure.
22
a clear bottle is an ethereal treasure.
23
empathy for the witches.
24
the island of lost lunatics.
25
let's have a period party.
26
"the pigs have won tonight."
27
"i hate you" is the new "i love you."
28
"the story of an hour" is read in queer time.
29
who is john waters?
30
her holy water stains the walls and doors.
31
a big mac makes up for tardiness.
32
"fuck" can be used to fill every part of speech in our grammar book.
33
she will kick your ass in heels.
34
*a room of one's own* will be a toy room.
35
36 pills and peach snapps can go fuck themselves.
36
your 7:20 is my 4:20.
37
"same" is a word with no language.
38
sushi, more sushi, and happy birthday!

## Professor St. Edmund

She has cysts on her head that explode with fiery ideas, professing glow words like pop rocks. She spits decaf like a tie-dyed dragon, flashing double middle-finger stares at passer-bys not in on the secret snicker. She has black nail polish on her jazz hands, speckled with earthy scents to be savored with licks. She bruises chests with love bites like her lead foot destroys her bumper below her skull plate. She has nipples that harden with tender touches, cuming on official biz in squirt series. She swipes keys like kisses inside during a fire drill, gunshotting her own smoke signals. She wags her ass like a swirl goddess, demanding spanx. She has dimples that dance, grinding in deviant tune to dots that connect. She locks arms in mid-air, skipping down the hall past the banal (not blue) blazers. She has hands that pull short hair, raising her mothering hips to the red flame. She curses adeptly, annunciating "fuck" like a gutter punk before a seventeen dollar word. She has eyelashes that make silent noise, fluttering butterfly kisses. She could learn how to swim, but prefers to soar underwater like a seagull skinny-dipping in sister sunset's love.

## Attraction

purely delusion,
bundles of holes, molecules,
nevertheless, always thinking,
dreaming of
( ).

# G Major

her moon eyes scream synonyms of desire,
reverberating off blackboards,
like heat on breath. she
tightens her.
she sucks the blood that drips,
catching it with her tongue. her
tongue slivers inside, harmonizing
in G minor.

# The Push Archives, Box I-III

Box I

*The Groundhugger and the Mudroller*

Hands webbed like sap-drenched leaves, the moist of a dreamlover dried up. The soil, which slid through the binocular hole of her hand, clogged in her fist like words written in haste in wet cement, unable to see. She hits the ground, one foot planted on the mud- caked hill, the other rests on her sunburned knee, unwanting to flee. She remembers unpetted names should never be carved onto an unpapered tree. She looks through the green fan of branches to the blue cool of the clouds, waiting to feel free. She steeps her tea, huffing the steam as a reminder that even a death breath in the deep woods has a right to be.

\* \* \*

Box II

*The Starkisser*

She wonders if this is it, the loss that actually makes her lose herself. She feels presence as a past. She heads to the dead. She stretches out on her grave at twilight. Her head touches the cold tombstone in the summer breeze, seeking warmth of a different kind, her sole feminist legacy. She feels the softness of the grass. It cradles her. She hears the cricket chorus. It soothes her. She elevates her head, reaching for the stars. She studies their language in the order of things, listening for some meaning outside of herself. They twinkle, fade, and dart across the black sky. Her breathing slows. She hears deer on the move. She blows kisses to the stars as her sweet dreams. She still feels their white fire.

\* \* \*

Box III

*The Dead Possum*

She stays in bed all day and night. She closes the curtain. She watches the sun rise and set in the same place through the small space. She smells the dead possum in the trash on the other side of the wall where life continues. She thinks it must have crawled in the garbage can to die. She does not have it in her to go out and deal. She stares at the closet in front of her. She took the doors off all of them. She likes the ease and air of the open. She realizes that the decay is trapped in there. She pulls the sheet over her nose. She remembers her sticking the sheet between her legs, leaving her sweet scent lingering in her smiles before slumber. She cries into the cotton cocoon, hoping for more than dead caterpillars.

# The Bark of Birch

the wind seen in drifts before crashes. the red leaves left crumbled. the sleet that hits ice monster geysters. the birch bark ripped by lyme-infested deer. the splintered shiver in wood stagnate. the frost that decapitates cattails. the cider breath on cracked windows. the curled finger with unmittened ink. the buck teeth that chatter in code. the paper airplanes headed to the glow below styx. the queen bumble bee in hibernation. the wild sweet pea in the tummy.

# Death Wish

She stomps in, like she was shot out of a canon, with her professorial bag slung over shoulder, dressed in a black tee and tight, blue jeans, hair pulled back tight. She makes classrooms sexy. She sees her at the front of the room, talking to her students, turns around, voice cracking, and encourages her students to go in, as she exits and hides outside somewhere in the halls. She stands there all swagged out, now stone as fuck, surreptitiously smiling inside herself that she is all hold back emo, spilling decaf coffee all over herself once again, still in love, though she tries to discipline herself against it. She imagines her dropping knowledge, as she emails her about lab logistics, cat condolences, and social media sophomorics just ten minutes into her class. It's been a month and a half since she gazed into her golden eyes, bit her right cheek off, ran her little fingers through her cysty hair, threw her left leg over her, caught her morning goodbye jump, and laced her sausage fingers in hers. She will flow in and out of her like the blood they swapped, noting I love you, let me kill you, no transfusion needed.

## Teasips

the subtle steep of bag
like air between bodies about to collide the
strum of the cat whiskers
like a harp
the trudge through hot air like a
blow dryer to the face the still of
the leaves
before     the     shattering
unleash     the     hydrants
hose the cement
the steam now rises like
heat from tea it's clearing
up there just above

# Dogwood

She started looking up Maple's skirts that summer. She would hit the ground without looking like collapsing in bed with whiskey on her breath. She would trace branches with her hazel eyes like connecting zit scars up her small back. She would soar through to the open blue like bumblebees through beard clouds. She would block out words for chirps with her long, dark hair shielding vision like a sun sheet. She would feel grounded with her chest to the petal stank above for the first time since she started dirt-hugging the layers that separated those who could trim nails from those who could not. She would let her litanies of questions drift like zen voices in the quietest woods. She learned how to breathe, inhaling so her shoulder blades shifted the dusty earth into the slow blow. She now has detached under Dogwood's denim cuffs, a billet-doux with a whipple.

# Rose Petals on a Tree Trunk

They take in the photos she snapped at their sushi spot. They examine the one of their dimps out at her closed eyes, feeling the calm in there and then out fast like her squirts. They recall their hands over their eyes, spreading their fingers, and slowly letting the light back in. They think about the slight nod of her head, the lid that shuts gently. The sun slides in through the curtain, just like touch slides under the skin. Their index finger and inked up thumb resting on her tan cheek, her head leaning into the space between them. Her palm on their stubble chin, redirecting their eyes to her. Their arms zig zag into an X, a buried treasure they hunted for as a kid and gave up trying to find. What story does the body tell? The cheeks that wears tears, the lips that sneak tongues, the forehead that wipes away frowns. The breath tells a story. It goes out, moves about, circles around, and returns back down. The depth of the story. They plot. They tell a story in a dialogue of sighs. She has their words now. Will she share her hours?

# Cherry Blossom Branch

*"I find support for m/y arms on the gust of air under the trees where it blows m/e strongly. M/y forearms are raised, they return very quickly against m/y body, then they are raised anew, they fall back, and so on in sequence with my fingers of m/y hands outspread. At a given moment, all together, I take off from the ground, I feel the grass brush against m/y calves, at last I make it, I fly off. [. . .] I look at the clouds at the place where the sun fringes them. It is there I direct m/yself."*
—Monique Wittig, *The Lesbian Body*

*Driftwood*

*she looks into her eyes like driftwood*
*sandy brown, upturned, golden hazel*
*tucked in life of seaweed and shells*
*bobbed and basked*
*dipped and flipped in*
*the calm-in*
*lies the speckle that never dries*

\* \* \*

Dear Ram,

I still think about you sometimes. I think about the good. I stare at the ceiling, thinking about how you say "puppy," "kitty," "uh huh," and "yeah." I look up a tree, thinking about how you used to jump on me in bed after huffing linens and before leaving for work. I gaze out the subway window, thinking about the "fucking Bull," "I love you, fucker," "and "my sweet Bull" notes you would leave in my home and office. I look at the ocean's waves, thinking about your windshield gifts—markers, napkins, "Nice" bottles, parking ticket "xo's." I look at the clouds, thinking about all the writing we did while we were together and for each other, including the writing and reading we did for my book. I glance at a red light, thinking about seeing you teach and say to your class, "is anybody sweating?" I look at the stars, thinking about your little feet pointed on the floor, your raised cheek, and the cysts on your head. I remember your blood is in my veins from when we swamped it, post-break up. I sit here thinking and sorting your writing. Sit here with what remains—letters, cards, post-its, schedules, receipts, among other mementos. Sit on my lap, surround the sides of me, barely at my feet. Sit here on a carpet island with you. Others visit, too, but they move, scatter about, and turn over with the breeze the window welcomes in. Some fly back at me and slap me in the face. Sit here with me. What do I do with these memories? How do I hold them in these hands? Read them, clutch them, smile at them, cry on them, mull on them, write back to them, toss them, burn them, just re-file them? Sit here holding. I miss so many beautiful qualities in you, the amazing moments we shared together, and how hard we loved each other those years. Sit here forgetting. I sit here remembering—the lives in them—yet letting go—the pasts in them. Sit here remembering-forgetting, forgetting-remembering.

* * *

### When Plastic Melts

*warm facial air like a*
*blow dryer*
*plug sparks shooting up that*
*summer car-time, floating*
*around like a balloon*
*wizened unblown up*
*about to graze mat*
*pebbles fossilized in*

*key cranked*
*down, down*
*not yet broken off blue*
*foamed,*
*a mouth hanging out inside*
*her upper arm antique*
*skeleton key tat marking up*
*whiteboards cables that drip*
*the battery*
*all still, with heat,*
*where grandmother's hands sat*

* * *

I still think about you sometimes, but I also think about the bad. I used to cry into my cats' bellies, thinking about you telling me "you are dramatic," "you are too sensitive," and "you are a baby." I used to cry into my pillows, thinking about you leaving me on the NYC sidewalk when your ex found us after Tegan and Sara while the next day I did your portfolio. I used to cry in my car on long trips upstate, thinking about you fucking your ex who wanted me dead, noted in the police reports, while I was jerking off to you in my tent and bawling my ass off in Fest's Oasis. I used to cry on hikes deep in the woods at Minnewaska, thinking about you on vacation with your ex while I was getting inked up for six hours just to feel. I used to cry in my yard looking at a bluebird, thinking about you fucking a stranger in a bar without protection while I was crying into the sand and with my shades on in front of friends at Riis and Fire Island. I used to cry in a fetal position on my bed, thinking about you not wanting me near your kids, your family, in your pictures, and in your life in any integrated way, owing to your internalized homophobia and coming out process. I used to have panic attacks, headaches, blackouts, and nightmares, spinning out in Triggerland of unaffection, unacknowledgement, and unworthiness. I remember how it felt to be out of my body—my neck jacked up, my legs cinder blocks, my stomach in knots, and my eyes all bagged up—and my focus gone to the point where I would walk into traffic without looking, because I was out of my mind, thinking about you so much that I lost my center, though it felt like home, the emotional abuse I experienced in my family growing up as a girl and on the street later for my genderqueer identity. I seldom cry about you now, but when I do, it is in the hammock alone or in somatic therapy, thinking about the ultimatums I dished out, the break ups I initiated, the threats I made, the critiques of parenting I made, the unacceptable treatment I dished back at you for the unacceptable treatment you hit me with from y/our closeted beginning, the abusive responses I chose to managing complex trauma. I loved you with all of my heart. I know you felt the same. However, you abused me bad, and I abused you back. We abused the hell out of each other. We loved each other the best we could with our past lives of trauma and without ways to cope, but it was not enough.

\* \* \*

*Deciding to Die (for Dorothy Allison)*

*Like blades of grass, her red arm hair bends, peaking out of the black cuff. Coattails propellered out, cheeks pulled back, it pushes her out the thirty-fifth floor window, flung like slingshot rocks bouncing off of apartheid walls that divide homes and hearts. Face smashed in the asphalt, head tilted with eyes sunken into her skull, with no hang time to float, she stares at the body that once carried her. Hands deep in denim pockets, wide Ramones' stance, she leans against the brick wall, leg kicked back, lifting her up, and she closes her eyes, sucks in her breath, releases it to the spores, and turns away from all that has haunted her. She steps on the cracks about which she obsessed yet in which she was entrapped, stretching her spine from side to side for the nervous system to thrive, while she shakes her shattered tooth in her hand like a die.*

\* \* \*

I still deal with the loss of you sometimes. I go to two trauma therapists each once a week, sometimes twice. I do yoga in a hammock every week. I decompress, cocoon, do the child-pose to stretch my spine, let my nervous system relax, Bessel van der Kolk- style, and let go of the trauma I am not carrying in the present. I do it every day in my home now. I do rapid eye movement, create containers made of glass bottles in seventies men's suitcases, and establish safe spaces of Amazon archers, greenhouses with cat caretakers, and circles of queer feminist friends and my new chosen family. I tap myself bilaterally—feet, legs, and hands. I do that every morning and every night. I sometimes do it before meetings when I know I will see you, after seeing you in the halls, in the lots, and at marches, as well. I have been in trauma therapy for a half a year. I meditate against walls, trees, and cats. I put one hand on my heart and one on my head to maintain peace and balance. I do that every morning and every night. I breathe deeply by the water at work. I do that three times a week before or after I teach. I write a gratitude list of at least ten things every day. I have done that for more than a half a year. I write about my trauma and how to get through it, usually at the end of the week or during creative writing workshops. I am grieving you—you, the living—but like with death, I am working through it to get to a better place within my new self / love.

\* \* \*

### Dead Woman's Float

I
*She awakes, rolls over, and rises up, knowing that she must go there to be touched without hands.*

## II

*She traces the hawks gliding along the route and feels the air between her fingers, whistling between peace signs.*

## III

*She listens to mind over matter and smells the patchoulied sunflowers bobbing about in the corn fields.*

## IV

*She snakes up the mountain and dips into the green without looking like a bad habit just below the limestone cliffs.*

## V

*She floats and lets the water rock-swish her into the present, where trauma no longer lives in the moment of un-being.*

## VI

*She feels the bubbles on her face soak into her pours and lifts her arms into full on Jesus Christ pose, letting the sun flow in.*

## VII

*She pushes away the hard water as if untangling herself from wild weeds and views the light streaming in through the leaves, finding a way to push on.*

## VIII

*She breathes in the scattered clouds whose patterns soon drift to form a rib cage once soft deep in, but now hard deep out.*

## IX

*She cradles herself into Minnewaska's cocoon pose, where she is un-becoming into her new seven year cells.*

## X

*She smiles thinking about her during adult swim doing the back stroke, wings soaked and still, flying above her with the butterflies going somewhere into the unknown.*

* * *

I am aware of our patterns now. I know you really well, Ram. I know what barging into my space and wanting help with a coming out flyer, looking for your pictures, and sticking your tongue out at me means. I know what "my sweet girl's smooth body," "my beautiful Bull," and "we are in love" revisions to your writing mean. I know what saying "hi," coming up to me in the hall, and flipping your hair mean. I know what tailgating me on the highway after a meeting before therapy means. I know what "proud" emails after a presentation mean. I know what your Slope memories following my request for professional boundaries means. I know what a handwritten letter and Altoids in my mailbox mean. I know what "good wishes" emails to both me and to family during the holidays mean. I know you regret it, but cannot check your ego, be direct, live unapologetically, or resolve conflict in a healthy way due to your own familial and marital trauma. You are still inviting me in the hurtful ways we showed love for each other. However, after we broke up and as soon as I started trauma therapy, I made a choice to see the possibility of love that is not mixed with so much hate, that hate and hurt and disavowals of love are not a necessary part of love, that love can be protective, that I must protect myself without hurting you, and that I will be open to new beginnings with a foundation of respect and equality. As a result, our past patterns do not engage me anymore. I did not know how toxic the push/ pull dynamic was when we were together, but I know it is now. I will never reproduce it again. I have no tolerance for manipulation, harassment, abandonment, and mind games now. I value emotional honesty, deep intimacy, non-reactive response, conflict resolution, and self-work and growth. I am more comfortable identifying and managing my triggers to poverty, domestic violence, alcoholism, street harassment, death, and break up traumas. I changed myself because I was tired of my shit and how I took it out on others, including you, for which I am deeply and eternally sorry, because I did not want to hold onto this tension, because I value self-respect just as much as romantic respect now, because my heart will beat wildly, both fully and healthily, soon—and it is pumping back harder each day for love that stays, gives back, and grows, individually and collectively. You were right—I did need to work on myself—bad. I really like how I am now. I feel happy, peaceful, grateful, stimulated, and fulfilled. I put this positive energy into the world, knowing I am worthy of love and devotion with vulnerability and intimacy, and I will be patient for it. I feel confident to feel and deal with any stress in life in healthy ways. I am excited to see even more progress after another half a year. I wish you would do the same. I wish I could give you even one minute of feeling what it is like to be me now. I feel safe inside myself. I know the difference between fighting and asserting, between hurting you to protect myself so I can be myself, and just being myself without needing protection, without the automatic reflex of fighting and hurting and pushing away and feeling that I have to fight to be myself. I feel terrible you seeing your emotional wounds without management skills. You have experienced so much trauma from your parents, your suicide attempt, your exes, including me, your kids, and your own coming out experience. You deserve the peace I have found.

* * *

### In the Hammock (for Karen Minsberg)

*to be supported the*
*ceiling above hooked in*
*all is gone*
*underneath it all*

*to be in the blue the*
*silk around*
*unweighed in all is here inside*
*just me*

*to be in the inhale the*
*hold back checked in*
*all is still out*
*it goes*

*to be in the crack the*
*release side tapped in*
*all is loose*
*open*
*like her mouth*

*to be on the other side the*
*step out*
*grounded in all is*
*smiles*
*like grabbing hers.*

* * *

I know today is your birthday—what used to be my favorite holiday. In this age of Trump, we all need to have more compassion towards each other, so I hope today starts off your new year in all the right ways for you. I hope you find yourself—if we ever fully do. I hope you have a closer connection with your kids. I hope your dog gives you his paw. I hope your cat kicks around a straw. I hope you have some slamming pasta, a salty skirt steak, an extra dirty Martini, blast the Ramones' birthday song, and I hope you are with loved ones around whom you can smile and laugh. I hope you get all that you wish for and more in life, Ram, and I hope you wish the same for me. I have given birth to a new me, both feet on the ground, my spine against a chair, my hands on my legs, drum-tapping away, and I look forward to the deep-breathing in new life, light, and love. I am sending you cherry blossoms in spirit.

Love,
Bull

\* \* \*

*5:27 Sherman*

*it shifts, the*
*focus,*
*just like that—eyes*
*extra white, bark-*
*brows*
*a flared up nose on a tree*
*drawn in.*
*sunflowers*
*single, then bunches, long*
*stretching heads to the sky*
*under-passing the grey.*
*much light-er.*
*they went unnoticed for*
*months, years. now*
*things just*
*pop up, looking up,*
*down the sidewalk. the*
*where*
*right there in*

*that—that gift,*
*that present, in*
*that—that just is.*

**VII.**

# Little Snowflakes

*A typical snow day as a kid*

My sister would pounce on my bed, announcing that school was closed in an imperialistic Paul Reveresque way. I'd jump up, wiping the sleep from my eyes and start bed-jumping and giggling with her to celebrate. My mom, a late-shift nurse, would wake up groggily and overdress us to the point where we hobbled like penguins and then we'd dart to the door, ready to embrace the snow. Once outside, my cat, Hepzebah (my sister's cat, Chloe, would never do anything fun) would follow us, as she did to the bus and friends' homes, etc. She always would drop in the snow, with us rescuing her by the sound of her frightened meows, lying underneath in an oddly enclosed cave. Hepzebah, learning from her error, would watch from afar on the porch, as we went sleigh riding down the massive hill in front of our home on garbage lids. My sister and I always seemed to be the first out, but, later, my best friend would accompany us.

We'd do all sorts of silly, fun-filled activities besides sleigh riding. For instance, we'd climb atop our swingset, doing flips and dropping into the snow after it, as one would do a bellyflop into a pool. A favorite one is me dangling from my underwear on a loose hook. It was painful, terrifying, and vexing—they roared with laughter, while I suffered from a first-rate wedgie, frostbite, and ridicule. Now it is quite humorous to me, especially since they only left me there for under a minute. We'd retreat to cornfields behind my friend's home, too. The cornfields were populated by green corn, deer, and a treehouse. We'd throw green corn at each other, socialize with the deer, and confess secrets in the treehouse. We loved the solitude and adventure, even though it was just behind her home. Then we'd get cold and would go inside for hot cocoa and cartoons. Then do it all again until it got dark.

\*\*\*

*A typical snow day as a teen*

I'd slam my hand down on my alarm clock. I'd get up quickly. I'd peer out the window, savoring the silence of the snow with Hepzebah, purring beside me in delight, before listening to the radio. Once I heard the good news, I'd drift back to sleep, usually after jerking off, and wake up a couple hours later. After I was officially up, I'd call my friend and go up to her house up the street, escorted by Hepzebah. We'd throw on Tori Amos' *Little Earthquakes,* flop onto her bed, and we'd brush each other's hair, sometimes dozing off, in between our interminable chatter for the duration of the day. I'd brush her hair with every ounce of me I had, and she'd do the same to me. The memory of it satisfied me in ways that were ineffable then.

***

*The last snow day as a het*

It was christmas. My partner and I stayed in bed. It snowed—and it snowed hard, almost ten inches were on the ground. We were saved! We loathed x-mas, as we do all holidays and things centered on consumerism and religion. We rejoiced after the cancellation, virtually unheard of in Irish families. We drifted off into the land of the zzzzzzzzz's again, with my leg over his leg, my arm over his, inseparable in our warm. I woke him up, and we talked, fucked, and snuggled all day, with only a film break (we watched an international film called *Noi*). The memory of this time satisfied me in ways that were ineffable then, though unimaginable now.

# Cornfields

Behind your home were the cornfields,
a mysterious, fun adventure for us as kids.
We threw green corn, rolled around in their husks,
and then told contraband tales in the abandoned treehouse.

The cornfields also were an experimental adventure for me as a teenager,
inebriated and sucking down cigs in the woods,
which i hid from you, more protective than my mother. The
guys and i threw corn, rolled around in their husks, and then
got ripped in the abandoned treehouse.

The cornfields have been paved for suburban development,
a vacant lot, waiting to be filled with middle-class monotony.
But i walked behind there recently
without my beloved cat trailing me.

i still remember our times there.
i can't seem to forget them,
like catholic school prayers,
even after twenty-five years.

# Giant Sleeping Beauty


we did them both
—about 6,500 feet—
back to back,
two of the Adirondacks.

the first was steep and taunting with multi-layers one
over
another
over
another
like corpses piled high in mass graves, but
with breaks until the summit, carrying our
heavy backpack,
while both of you sprawled out, tongues hanging out, panting like dogs on the
ground.

the next was gradual, easy
with
anti-capitalist conversations, Che's
aspirations and asthma, these
Dack-cake mountains.

## Photogenic Litter

i've known you for years, each
part of you,
pure limestone rock/ water & Maple trees, with
isolated, descending mini-caves,
a foot below the lookout, the
Gunks,
just a mile off of Jenny Lane before Lake Awosting,
acknowledged,
discarded,
littered with kodak wrappers,
protective like a middle-aged controlling father over
a teenage girl's nascent sexuality.
pick up, imagine
this, snap up
and secs. later kill
you.

# Red Catskills

All along Wittenberg i stared
at birds deer and leaves in a
trance
until i glanced
at my clayed sloes
d
       r
           i
                   p
                         p
                              i
                                  n
                                        g
red
focusing on colonized kids chucking rocks at tanks with each
step
throwing bricks at beehives is no way to live

# The Footnote

the ex who is not the et al
the remembering and footnoting
the subject who should be
the object of analysis
the citing
the forgetting
the archaic
the esoteric
the homophobic
the misanthropic
the static
the hidden materiality
the tangible antiquity
the back of the drawer smell
the door of the closet ajar
the history
the erasure
the way you want it to be
the ex who becomes the etcetera.

# A Portrait of the Marxist as a Commodity Identity

your framed ebay Marx stamps
fell
again
the other day behind the table
where you
broke its back
and left the
glass
for me to see
back there.
it falls a lot,
but i keep putting it up.
you (say you) don't care,
but i was always sympathetic to him,
despite his myriad silences.

his stamps join the fragments of you—
stubs of old digits, pad addresses, snug certificates, fake, plastic bills, 1040s,
subversive flyers,
(un)voting cards, bank statements, unemployment forms, pill bottles, Mexico
blankets, Paris art,
*Phoblacht na hÉireann* reproductions, Hellmark cards, preamble letters, hand-
written guided by
voices labels, nelson *ok computer* software, student against empire pilgers, and
*eternal sunshine-*
your possessions are shattered everywhere.

the materiality of Marx—
all i have left of my Marxist ex
lies in the (broken) silence of possessions,
only spoken through the (fixed) poetry of my voice.
antithesis and antithetical—
they are all that is
left of my leftist
ex.

# Whisker Gifts

nothing beats writing indoors at
the Lux-Volt Compound,
with my dusty charcoal, grey sweatpants, moon-eyed,
with my white-nosed tiger, dolphin tail dipped in paint, owl-eyed,
radical feminist cats
on the table
next to my warm cpu,
petting them
in between paragraphs,
punctuated with purrs,
boomerangs,
and whiskers.

# Enjera

I.
She met her on 14th and U, just off the metro across from Ben's Chili Bowl, with all its grease and all its riots, not far from the most unimportant house in the country. She was late, a genetic defect, distracted by the stillness of words. She met her atop the escalator, towering over her with smoke lassoing them before arms welcomed smiles, curved like cantaloupe wedges. They shared Almaz Ethiopian Restaurant's vegan combo for two, loaded with lentils, string beans, potatoes, and cauliflower. No fishy business. They fumbled for food, grazing the soft life between each other's fingers. She imagined sucking her fingers one at a time, as if they were the right sulci of her brain. Their eyes protested blinks, their minds syncing metaphors. She went to the only bathroom with two toilets in a one stall. She felt her eyes undress her before she released the toxic she was holding in. Her knees welcomed her back, but then buckled when leaving. The Gold Star Taurusian and the Aqueerian, they broke Enjera.

II.
They plopped on the couch to watch a film about women in the FMLN. There is a habitual in the inceptional. She traced her tattoo on her hand, and then she the punched the "off" button. They courted clits and cradled cervixes for fourteen hours, two shifts in cuntsciousness. No dating, no "i love you-ing," no uhaul-ing, where the tactile and auditory coalesce, whisper touches. The mired and the admiring, the sharing intrigue and the awaken fatigue, existed in circles. Half-circles, which never want to become full-circles, are inherently complete. The Cunticles continued through the eclipses, the new *amor* in the old lunar. Her gold stars were out. Double the digits in dyke-time, nine months, like cat-years. She eventually got the bottom drawer, with the cat's permission, but her one hand still held onto to the Big Apple, the other onto He(r)art. She wrote her "I love you's" on her lips, pursing her lips until the *Éire* research departure. She crygasmed dire—the fire of desire or the home with swing of tire—the point of mire. She left her job for her, prop master imagination to grad school application. She sustained her until grounded. Home is not a place of yearning, but the being in belonging. Home is the here in her.

III.
We met almost a half a decade ago. Since I met you, I have been able to tie my shoes to the perfect level of tightness. You snug-tug my shirts and texture up my pants. I tickle and caress your tiny feet like your grandmother did. You big-

toe me and hold the cats' paws. I tuck you into bed and make up slumber party stories that make you snort-laugh. You run your hands through my (un)loced hair that makes dead matter dance. I make figure-eight patterns on your back with my snowfingers. You compare the contrast in our skin. I think no one peels my sunburn better than you. Awe, I adore the way you draw Womyn, the Wind, and the Whiskermen. "Allthetime," you fast-talk like a little kid walking on tippy toes when I poem for and about you. We line up our dimples, just like we line up our clits. We get separation anxiety when we cannot hold hands under bathroom stalls. We embrace openness as a place where door knobs become bra holders.

We trade kisses like baseball cards. We bounce around ideas like blowing bubbles, laughing when deliberating makes them pop. We now break Enjera from the nest, not Almaz but Ghenet, where the past and present meet, the sloths of the future rest.

# The Wise Clock

We are at the people's beach. The sun photographs us without red i's. Seagulls share cheese doodles. We sit in the ungentrified north. Hair dyes make rainbows. The waves rise hey there's and roll bye-bye now's. They erase breast impressions. Our breathing slows. My chin rests on my hand. She sips her lemonade. Our toes exchange sand gifts and then lock thank you's. i feel time's abolition here. i recall Prue. We all die in parentheses. i feel the wind and ask her, "What are we supposed to do with this life thing?" She looks at the sea, smiles, and says, "Finish our lemonade."

# VIII.

# The Raven and the Wren

*"[W]e're out in a country that has no language/ no laws, we're chasing the*
*raven and the wren."*
      —Adrienne Rich, "Twenty-One Love Poems, XIII"


I rule out laws like meter. I piss in the men's bathroom at the opera. And I can
start and end a line with "and." I used to hock a loogie as I crossed the street or
side-eye my way up it. I up my swag and let my black knife and skull crowbar
keychain protrude in my pocket now. I recall the guy who threw coffee at me
on the way to the barber. Recall the guys who grabbed my bike, my throat, and
my cunt to find out if I had one. The way the airport security guy looked you
up and down from behind as you walked away from him in your unicorn dress.
Your nightmare of dudes chasing us in the woods. I make sure my cats sleep
near me, not having too much to fear-dream at night. I refill your water cup
on your side as I return from my night pee. I do not invite strangers into my
sentences. I spread out my words like air. I invent this world without husbands
and caesuras. I wonder how people read you/ me - us/ them together, and then
I realize I write with double middle fingers in the sun anyway. I read herstories
and theirstories, but I imagine our scrolls written with our tongues and without
genres in exile.

# The Socratic Circle

> "Perhaps the world will end at the kitchen table, while we are/ laughing and crying, eating of the last sweet bite."
> —Joy Harjo, "Perhaps the World Ends Here"

The object/ive of affect, the subject imagines. Flicking a cig in a gentrified puddle, skipping a pebble on a frog-squatted lake, kicking dirt off a fall cliff, rolling a marble off a glass table, cat-swatting a paper clip across the tiled floor. The lack of matter, the subject wonders. The point of a running start to chuck an apple in an open orchard, as opposed to a wind up pitch without meatheads catching. The difference between stomping a fag into the cement with queer boots, as opposed to dabbing it and carrying it back, avoiding urban littering. Opposing as, as opposed, as detaching from syntax/ meaning, the shadows with no matter, the child shares his ponderings, as he skips with them over sidewalk cracks. The subject moves the objects about like pronouns. They out. The name changed out, the chest not out, the one evicted out, the ones with lilies in intestines pulled out, and ones, post- slaughterhouse, casts smiling out. The subject of the sanctuary. The goat therapy there. The child's shoulder propped up on their back, holding her face, shouts out, "Red, I want to live here." The subject/ive traces clouds, shapes-shifts in the hay, the wonder under them.

# Smash, the Swoon Falconer and Moon Witch

***

She pulls her hair back. She leans against her Falcony fence. She takes a drag. She stares at them and smiles. They stand with their leg kicked up against her wall. They feel the wind on their face. They look into her eyes and smile back. They move towards her. They pull her burgundy hair and then grab her smile. They feel it cupped in their hand. She blushes and turns her head. She smiles harder, takes another drag, and wraps her foot around them. They lift her onto the metal ridge that separates her cat from water bugs, kiss her hard, run their hands along her inked up back and shoulders, feel her skin crawl, feel the warmth under her unicorn dress and her lace panties, watch her tilt her back and hear her moan softly, smoke lassoing us in, and think about leaping off the roof like jumping on her bed on top of her with her altar of witchy candles flickering behind them. They think about how their smile has returned unexpectedly, an uninvited guest to whom they offer tea and encourage to sit on their couch.

***

She sits next to them on the bench by Prospect Park in the fall chill after leaving the Archives. She is wearing her leather jacket, feather earrings, and pink lipstick, her black bag beside her to keep her belongings accessible and safe. They look up between the trees by the F train. They feel burning in them. They ask her if they can smear her lipstick. She wipes it off with her fingers. They kiss hard. Their hands twirl her hair. Their legs levitate, their neck hairs rise, and their junk is throbbing. They see the pre-supermoon on her blushed up face. She smiles, slinks back into the bench, smiles harder. They feel their shaved skull, just as like their binder, vest, and leather jacket are strangling their chest off. Instead, they dig their wallet into the wood, they pull her into them, thinking about that rather than clutching their knife as they chainsmoke on the way home.

***

They have been here before. More than once. Queers and hubs. Right to left. Oh, chiseled-hearted one, then. Crane around. Not so now. Stone. In a shared room. Heat-slashing knives. On her tummy. Neck jammed up. Fuck stiffening up. Look up. Sometimes. Up a tree. A Catholic girl's skirt. Just cloud-drift it. Suck in. A red leaf rains down. In open palm. Come down. Curl up. This is. Ground. Hair brushed dirt. Planes at fingerpoint. Blow with them. Through the lightning. Unicorns fly on and around. Ride on. Her. They have been here before. Now twice, thrice. They remember hugging away his tears away at the circus, cuddling him to sleep in Northampton, skipping rocks and swapping stories at Pond Eddy, feeding the goats together and taking pictures of him at the Woodstock Sanctuary, seeing the art he made in school at the Rubin, surfing down the volcano with him in Nicaragua, finding secret shortcuts in the woods at Sisterspace with him, riding bikes and scooters with him in Brooklyn, and listening to him talk about how g-o-d does not exist in the tub with his vegan soap. Plus another. They have not been here before. Kids, not this time.

# Tenderstorm

I picture you curled into a corner of a couch, legs up as a shield, as you drop the deal and dodge the sharp. I lie in the grass with my cats, back sunken into the dirt, as I think about sunrises. Let me be soft with you now. Let me tuck you in, spooning you up as I smile-stamp my stubble and freckles into your birthmarked back. Let me stare at a dark ceiling, feeling your sleep twitches and listening to your sleep noises as I slow-breathe in your taste on the way to our willow dreamland. Let me wake up to the warmth of your chest smashed up into my face, your nipples etched into my cheeks, as I inhale your sleep sweat under there. Let me kiss you with our morning breath, caress your peace-lips, twirl your night-sex hair, and draw double Z-whiskers on your hungry tummy. Let me use my hands longer to rub your neck, to wash your hair, to add more soy creamer to your coffee, to hold your sleepover bags, and to hold your hand the whole drive back to your pad. Let me look into your sleep-filled eyes in queer trust. Let me try to be as soft as I can in the hard of it all for now.

# Flor de Cana Swing

\*\*\*

I pull it. In the supermarket, I pull it, the cart with the mac 'n cheese, Ben 'n Jerry's, chicken nuggets, and other foods I do not eat, one kid on one side and one on the other. I am looking for you in each aisle. I powerwalk up and down the store, I zig zag around the sale displays, and spin the cart in circles, around and around, faster and faster, the harder they laugh. I see your smile in theirs. The shy laugh when I call you hot in the sunlight. The excited laugh when I pull your face into mine. The badass laugh when I grab your hair. The eccentric laugh when I tell you self-care is sexy. The absurd laugh when my cats are purring and snoring. The orgasmic laugh when the gummies kick in at roundabouts. And the silent laugh when I tell you I am grateful you are here. The lows and highs of them. Where you release sound when you cannot speak it. Why it sits here in this room with no penises—just a shadow of them. When you hear the laugh hit the door like a tampon, knocking harder.

\*\*\*

In between the sun and the ground, the shadows illuminate. Crescents sway, almost weightless, like swimming on cement—miniature eclipses with little light. I glance down at my tired feet, planted atop the moon energy. I feel the dark shifting under me, the soil loosing under the grey layer holding me up. Sometimes I need to look down to look up. I think about Andrew's words about weeds, the "life genius" that grows in the pavement below the drainage pipe that waters it.

\*\*\*

The trees blow more freely; they have massive roots protruding with aging roots here. The fireflies beam light an extra two of three more hits. The birds glide along the water with longer hang time. The FSLN flags fly backwards and circle around to view unphotogenically. The kids bounce on trampolines, fly through the air on tree-swings, and jump into the unmonitored waves. The government provides wifi and electric trees along the highways. What does it take to let my back free up now? I dream about simulacra. It's gutted from an earthquake that still shakes a cathedral from four decades ago. It's the poverty of oranges, this being.

***

I coasted down the zipline and screamed down a volcano-boarding adventure with your son. I befriended the pregnant dog and watched your three hands pet the new pups. I remember you looking at monkeys—your teeth fully out, the directness of your gaze, your head tilted back, wide like a rainbow. I breathe in the air where all the dying preying mantises were in Nicaragua before I drift into sleep.

***

She tells me to find her under the willow tree before she drifts off to sleep. She tells me what she is wearing—purple hoodie, lion t-shirt, and leopard pants. She dreams of turtles in Nicaragua in the summer. Awake, the dry mouth was real. They are in the woods with robes on, but under different willows. How did those willows take her kids from me?

IX.

# Feminist (Un)Apology

I'm sorry, but I'm not sorry.
She knows they suffer from walls built
with insidious patriarchal tools artificial
barriers chiseled in ideologies stronger
than columns she muscles her mired
mind
off the straight line
swooping zigzagging
levitating
from corners
the weeds in cement
floating to the summit
blanketed in sunflowers that drip with dew
looking down
another angle of vision
she smiles between her fingers
the spaces that now sense how small that
life is
below.

# Big Ol' Amerikan

cruisin' in my big ol' suv,
chowin' down on my big ol' big mac,
prayin' to my big ol' almighty, watchin'
my big ol' flat-screen tv, blastin' my big
ol' toby keith, sportin' my big ol' yellow
ribbon, sayin' "love it or leave it,"
i'm a good ol' amerikan.

# Amerikan Hypocrisy

Oh, say, can you see?
The supposed land of the "free?"
Free to shop 'til you drop and go into debt. Free to watch t.v. and devalue intelligence.
Free to follow orders from the (corporate) state, military (murderers), & police (screws). Free to regurgitate false amerikan history (and believe amerika = #1—u$a, u$a, u$a!!!) Free to be racist.
Free to be classist. Free to be sexist.
Free to be heterosexist. Free to be ethnocentric. Free to be transphobic. Free to be Islamophobic. etc, etc, etc.
Free to hate      the rest of the world. Free to be ignorant.
Free to not even know what we are celebrating.


Oh, say, can you see?
How proud we are of our sanitized history.
Proud of the so-called "founding fathers" gracing your bills—
American Indian killers, slaveowners, misogynists, rich-landowners who raped, pillaged, stole.
Proud of their declaration of independence—their freedom to consolidate capital without the crown.
Proud of the wars (you) fought for imperial expansion—Spanish-American, the Philippines, Korea,Vietnam, Iraq, way too many to count on their (your) bloody hands. Proud of the wealth of the elite (for which you worked)—
ford, carnegie, rockefeller, gates, buffet, the waltons, and other capitalists.
Proud of the undemokratic (plutocractic) government (over which you have no influence)—demokrats
(republikans?), republikans (demokrats?), kongress, supreme kourt, executive (monarch?) Proud to not even know what we are celebrating.

## The Mount of Flags

the clouds open,
the lightning whispers, the
thunder screams,
all pouring themselves out,
moving in electric dissension
to their similar points of (dis)interest—
u$ red-baiting, streaming letters and Cuban black, starred flags—camouflaging
them.

it hits me,
not like a flash of lightning on the queerish waterfront, but
rather like a sting of an ant in the yucca fields. they both
crackle and murmur—
the fire and light of the past and present. i
stand there
soaked in the dew's sorrow, weeding
and resisting the forgetting
of the fruits of labor in the tropical zone—
Fidel, Che, Raul, Haydee, Cecilia, Tania.

the scent of mangos lingering,
like cohiba tobacco to palm trees in factories,
 intoxicating-yet-blockaded.
when will my people stand here in the rain with me
barefoot on its crushed-resurrected grass,
and the feel the dripping nectar
down
cheeks and chests onto
the blood and sweat of
the ground?
the sun still rises here.

## Ivory Tower Utopia

a place where students,
hands on faces,
staring at walls, write
world wrongs with bloody stumps,
a place where students, feel
their mouths open
hear the sound of silent pasts
sharing bullet tear drops
with collective hugs and snaps
in classrooms constructed in circles,
where a dog laps up water
and strolls about upstairs, where
underneath professors
sit with them wearing vanilla ice cream mustaches,
curled towards the chandeliers and grand pianos,
unpacking Lorde, Mohanty, Rivera, Crenshaw,
Ahmed, Claire, and Puar,
where tongues feel teeth,
saying she/he/they
where they rip apart silly putty,
spitting their stories
of microaggressions during office hours, a
place where they climb a mountain with a
gallbladder out the next week,
where a professor's boot sole is thrown in the bushes, atop
an Afrofuturistic book sits at the cliff,
where a professor talks honestly about war trauma,
where research teaching fellows
hook up study sessions about race,
jump vans, call out privilege, sip and paint on weekends, dj
trips, and push for trans ally workshops,
where students talk about immigration and
then swim with the ducks who do not abide by bouy borders, and
eyes follow butterflies in sculpture gardens,
where research teaching fellows direct with
rebel cats meowing in the car
share out knowledge about indigenous lands

liberations that require another angle of vision,
where a professor pushes collaborative papers
and grades them with her sick daughter on her chest in a
setting focused on valedictorians,
where the chair and director drops knowledge about
the politics of voice in sweats and a t-shirt,
takes students to the dentist and ER in between classes,
talk about critical race theory over jackfruit potpies,
asparagus, and mashed cauliflower,
and bowls day one and
then gets down and belts out Adele with them at the end, a
place where our love feast comes with lemonade
a flowing during home office hours,
hammocks hold heads high
in the summer breeze
higher than we have been before.

X.

# COVID-19: Trans Lives and Trans Studies

*How are surviving pandemics and Transgender/Gender Nonconforming/Queer movements inter-connected?*

There have been many prior pandemics with many connections to LGBTQ communities. Naomi Replansky, a lesbian poet, age 101, has recently talked about embracing her confinement during the COVID-19 pandemic. She has reflected on living through the Spanish Flu, the Great Depression, and the Holocaust. The AIDS pandemic is often forgotten in the litany of pandemics. It is often portrayed as a gay disease by the mainstream media, but it has tremendously impacted women, including trans folks. Trans folks are very much a part of the AIDS pandemic, and are a vulnerable population within it without the same access to healthcare. I'm thinking about an ACT UP flyer that read "women don't get AIDS… they just die from it." These issues are resurfacing now, as we don't have the same healthcare access during the Trump administration as we did under the Obama administration. LGBTQ folks, historically, too, have been pathologized as "sick," "perverse," and "monsters." Mike Davis, an American scholar, political activist, and historian, recently discussed capitalism using the metaphor of the "monster," and the first thought I had was about trans folks, including folks with disabilities, being deemed "monstrosities." The DSM only recently removed Gender Identity Disorder from its manual, just a few years ago, for instance. COVID-19 expands pandemics created and exacerbated by capitalism and neoliberalism (as well as white supremacy and cis-heteropatriarchy) with its values of big pharma and prisons—profits and bailouts over people. Politicians and administrators often use sickness as a distraction with elections looming to promote their political agenda and fascist policies, how global warming is destroying land, animals, plants, and indigenous and two-spirit lives (for instance, I'm thinking about the Amazon), and how capitalism needs "disasters," what Naomi Klein calls "disaster capitalism," to thrive. Those folks especially targeted and harmed are those experiencing poverty, homelessness, starvation, unemployment/ job discrimination, lack of healthcare or access to decent healthcare, educational struggles, food/hunger, social stigma, etc. Trans people have high rates of all of the above, in particular, as well as social isolation from family/kin, friends, depression, suicide, anxiety, and hate violence, including from the state. Trans folks' politics of everyday life and frequent injustice and microaggressions are merely exacerbated and made hypervisible with the recent pandemic. Whose life matters? Who is essential? Who is a human? These are questions philosophers like Judith Butler and George Yancy have been asking as well as by addressed by activists in Black Lives Matter, led by Black queer women.

*Does the COVID-19 pandemic present a unique challenge for our communities?*

Yes. All the issues I mentioned are social justice issues that affect trans folks across the spectrum of difference. Some unique challenges coming up now include the 30 million people with no healthcare access, and those that do have it, often can't see doctors who treat them humanely—for example, don't want to touch or evaluate us—or have doctors who just can't see us for surgeries, hormones, etc., because of the quarantine. We can't go to court for name and gender changes. Lawsuits—including mine against my university—are on hold. These are some examples that can lead to increased violence that not only affects our physical health, but also our mental health. Trans folks are affected by intimate partner violence and toxic environments, are homeless/ kicked out when they come out/ are without work/ are sex workers and living on the streets, are in prison and solitary confinement, state-sanctioned social distancing (for example, Layleen Polanco died/ was murdered at Rikers and Chelsea Manning just released because of mental health reasons), are around transphobic families and housemates, and/or are dealing with cyber bullying from bosses and colleagues. I'm thinking of Lorena Borjas's death, which shows the intersecting realities of trans folks and the harm being enacted on individuals and our communities.

*What are our survival strategies?*

We were never meant to survive, as Audre Lorde reminds us. Our recognition as humans has been stripped from us during the Trump administration—from healthcare, to housing, to the military. It started with his removing us from the White House website on his Inauguration Day and removing non-discrimination policies from the Affordable Care Act. The Hungarian government seeks to end the legal recognition of trans folks during this crisis. To survive, we have had to create our own communities and organizations from Sylvia Rivera's and Marsha P. Johnson's work with STAR to Trans Lifeline. We survive in community. We dissociate to survive as well as create care and support networks because we do not have access to many services. We create our own families and housing. Survival is our resistance.

*In your teaching/ research/ advocacy how do you see transgender/GNC/*

*queer communities being impacted by the COVID-19 pandemic? What is your experience with teaching trans/studies "online"?*

In my Women's and Gender Studies classes, we have been talking a lot about rethinking knowledge and learning using multiple modalities and assessments/ grading methods as well as connecting them to rethinking single-issue struggles and moving towards multiple issues. We have been talking about how to create a better world in and outside of the classroom for folks who are targeted now, including poor, working-class, women, trans and nonbinary folks, lesbian, bisexual, gay, and queer folks, folks with disabilities and immuno-compromised folks, and/or elderly folks. In particular, we have been talking a lot about racism targeted against Asian Americans in my classes because of COVID-19. In class, I've also been talking about my own experiences with whiteness and privilege as a tenured professor with stable work and health benefits. I've shared my relief at having a shelter in a place that is safe, but my guilt thinking about prisoners (approximately 2 million in prison at high risk of infection) and homeless folks who are sick and dying. I've also shared my frustrations about lack of rights for delivery workers, doctors, nurses, and farmworkers, among others. I've also shared my relief about my experiences with less misgendering, less exposure to street violence, less bathroom policing, and less harassment at work during the quarantine. I've been relieved that many students with disabilities and/or many working-class students—mainly BIPOC students have access to the learning they should have received along with accommodations and technologies in place with remote learning. I've shared my concerns about not being able to see medical professionals about my own health issues during my transition. I've been inspired by the empathy, generosity, and kindness in my classes— how students are being emotionally supportive to each other. I've been most excited by the discussions about making a new world—general strikes, rent moratoriums, mutual aid for food and medical depositories, and fighting for people's right to a life in ways capitalism can't provide through its value of corporations, the destruction of the environment and indigenous communities, and the lack of stable work as the impact of COVID-19 takes us into a recession with rates of higher unemployment than the Great Depression. What does a world look like without exploitative work, carceral and detention institutions, and inflated rent/ gentrification, etc.? What are the possibilities of hope we can now create for a more just world? This is just the beginning of the current phase of the ongoing freedom struggle.

# ACKNOWLEDGMENTS

- "COVID-19: Trans Lives and Trans Studies." *Trans Bodies, Trans Selves: A Resource for the Transgender Community*. Ed. Laura Erickson-Schroth and Kevin Johnson. 2nd Ed. New York: Oxford, 2021.
- *Tit-Bucket and Denim: Trans Bodies and Friendship*. Photo Ed. Elektra KB. Brooklyn: Transgressive Cíborg Tekhnika (TCT), 2020.
- "Label Maker," "The Raven and the Wren," "The Socratic Circle," and "Nightfall." *Sinister Wisdom: A Multicultural Lesbian Literary and Art Journal. Forty-Five Years: A Tribute to the Lesbian Herstory* Archives, co-edited with Elvis Bakaitis and Shawn(ta)Smith-Cruz. (Fall 2020) 137-140.
- "Cliff Notes: On Memory, Identity, and Community." *Sinister Wisdom: A Multicultural Lesbian Literary and Art Journal. Moon and Cormorant*. Ed. Julie R. Enszer. (Spring 2019). 127-133.
- "Power, or Point of Zoo." *Sinister Wisdom: A Multicultural Lesbian Literary and Art Journal. Dump Trump: Legacies of Resistance,* co-edited with Cheryl Clarke, Morgan Gwenwald, and Stevie Jones. 110. (Fall 2018): 256-257.
- "Cherry Blossom Branch." *Sinister Wisdom: A Multicultural Lesbian Literary and Art Journal. The Lesbian Body*. Ed. Tara Shea Burke. 106. (Fall 2017): 54-64.
- "156 Avenue and Madison Road." *Sinister Wisdom: A Multicultural Lesbian Literary and Art Journal. Celebrating the Michigan Womyn's Music Festival*, co- edited with Angela Martin, Brynn Warriner, Shawn(ta) Smith-Cruz, and Allison Ricket, 103. (Winter 2017): 90-95.
- "Enjera." *Sinister Wisdom: A Multicultural Lesbian Literary and Art Journal. Reconciliations.* 95 (Winter 2015): 116-117.
- "What Is Felt There," "Macramé Keychain," "St. Francis," "Squire," "How Do You Love a Ghost," "Crestview Tree Woman," "Pretzel Cigars," "Sacred Heart," "Red Catskills," "The Footnote," and "A Portrait of a Marxist as a Commodity Identity." *Crestview Tree Woman*. Georgetown: Finishing Line Press, 2013.

Red Washburn, PhD, is Associate Professor of English and Director of Women's and Gender Studies at CUNY Kingsborough. They also teach Women's and Gender Studies at Brooklyn College and the Graduate Center. They are the co-editor of *WSQ*, published by the Feminist Press. Their book *Irish Women's Prison Writing: Mother Ireland's Rebels, 1960s-2010s* is forthcoming from Routledge. Finishing Line Press published their chapbook *Crestview Tree Woman.*

www.ingramcontent.com/pod-product-compliance
Lightning Source LLC
Chambersburg PA
CBHW021147090426
42740CB00008B/982